103 Low-Prep ESL Speaking Games & Activities for Kids, Teenagers, and Adults:

The Ultimate Book for Busy English Teachers

Jackie Bolen

www.eslspeaking.org

Table of Contents

4

About the Author: Jackie Bolen

I taught English in South Korea for a decade to every level and type of student, including every age from kindergarten kids to adults. These days, I'm living in Vancouver and teaching English to a variety of students. In my spare time, you can usually find me outside surfing, biking, hiking or on the hunt for the most delicious kimchi I can find.

In case you were wondering what my academic qualifications are, I hold a Master of Arts in Psychology. During my time in Korea, I completed both the Cambridge CELTA and DELTA certification programs. With the combination of years teaching ESL/EFL learners of all ages and levels, and the more formal teaching qualifications I've obtained, I have a solid foundation on which to offer teaching advice. I truly hope that you find this book useful and would love it if you sent me an email with any questions or feedback that you might have—I'll always take the time to personally respond (jb.business.online@gmail.com).

Jackie Bolen around the Internet

ESL Speaking (www.eslspeaking.org)

YouTube (https://www.youtube.com/c/jackiebolen)

Instagram (www.instagram.com/jackie.bolen)

Pinterest (www.pinterest.com/eslspeaking)

Introduction to the Book

I love to make learning English fun and interesting for my students. Happy, engaged students will remember the content far better than bored, disinterested ones! That's why I've written this book—to give other teachers some fun ideas to try out with their students.

Quite honestly, this is the book that I wish I'd had when I first started teaching. There just wasn't anything like this 20 years ago. Instead, I relied on *Dave's ESL Cafe* for some ideas for my classes, but it was quite difficult to find something that would work. I usually ended up making my own games instead.

Skip over the frustration and just use this book! You'll find 101 ESL speaking game and activity ideas that will ensure a great class. You should be able to find one that'll work for whatever you're teaching in just a minute or two. These games have been tried and tested over my teaching career and the result is things that work, in the real world—your classroom!

What this book isn't meant to do is replace a textbook. The games are not a comprehensive treatment of the English language. Instead, if you teach conversation or general English, I recommend using an appropriate textbook (I like "Let's Go" for children, and "4 Corners," "Smart Choice," "World Link," and "Touchstone" for adults) and then supplementing the lesson with one or two of these fun games. Perhaps use one as a warm-up activity at the beginning and then another as a review activity at the end. There are some activities that take up an entire class period, such as a review day before a test. Finally, you can find some "just for fun" activities that are ideal if you teach at a summer or winter camp, or just want to have a "party" day in class.

I hope this will be your go-to resource for all things ESL games and activities! There are a variety of activities that will work well for larger classes of 20+ students. All of them will work for smaller classes of 4-12 students. And many of them are ideal for private tutoring or online teaching as well. Many of them are based on pair work but in this case, the teacher can act as the partner for the student.

Who This Book is For

This book will be helpful for a wide range of people. Perhaps you're an experienced teacher, but are stuck in a rut when it comes to lesson planning and you feel like your teenage or adult students are not engaged in your classes. Or, maybe you're a very busy teacher with an extremely heavy teaching load and don't have a lot of time to plan your lessons. Maybe you have closely followed a textbook for all your classes up to this point, but you now have a class with no book and are trying to figure out what to do. You might also be an inexperienced teacher and you've only been teaching for a few weeks or maybe you've never set foot in an ESL classroom before. This book is for you!

Perhaps you've been searching the Internet, trying to find some new ideas for ESL speaking games and activities, but are tired of wading through haystacks of useless and poor search returns to find the needle that you can use in your class. This book is perfect for you too. My aim is that this will be an *extremely practical* resource to help make your speaking or conversation classes interesting and fun, as well as making your lesson planning quick and easy. I've written the book that I wish I had ten years ago when I first started teaching, and also one with content that I have been using all the years since then. Everything you see in this book has been tried in real-world classrooms and proven to work for myself as a teacher, and more importantly for improving the speaking skills of my English language learners.

This book will also be helpful for you if you find yourself thrown into a situation where you're given a new speaking class at the very last minute and there's nothing provided in the way of materials. This situation is all too common when working at a place like a cram school. The majority of the activities in this book truly are no-prep or low-prep and require almost nothing in the way of materials.

I hope this book is a resource that you'll refer back to again and again as you plan your ESL lessons and that it will make your teaching life easier.

ESL Speaking Activities for All Levels

Vocabulary Flip Chart

Skills: Speaking/listening

Time: 20 minutes

Materials: Flip-chart or

The captain sits in a chair at the front of the class facing her team. The teacher stands behind the captain with vocabulary words on a flip-chart or a stack of flashcards. If you use flashcards, make sure they are big enough for everyone to be able to see them, even at the back of the class. The team has to give hints in English (no gestures) to the captain until she can guess the word. At that point, the team moves on to the next word. Each round is three minutes and you can play 3-4 rounds with different captains. I give each group one pass per round in case there is a word that the captain doesn't know.

Teaching Tips:

One of the ways that students gain fluency is by employing communication strategies such as substitution, which means that when a student can't remember the specific vocabulary word that they want to use, they're able to substitute another word, or phrase to get their meaning across. This game is very useful for practicing substitution skills in a fun way.

Make sure you emphasize that this game requires speaking only English. It is too easy for students to say the word in the their first language, the captain says it in English and then it's not a useful speaking activity. I warn students at the beginning of the game that if I hear a word in their first language, that round will immediately finish, even if they are only 5 seconds into it.

One of the cons of this game is that the other team is sitting idly waiting while the other team is playing. A way to alleviate this problem is by keeping the rounds very short so that waiting time is reduced. You can also mention that any word that a team has "passed" on could come back into play so it's good to pay attention. Furthermore, elicit the other team's help to watch for any infractions such as gesturing, miming, or not speaking in English.

Procedure:

1. Prepare a large flip-chart of flashcards with the target vocabulary. I often use an old notebook.

2. Put the students into teams of 4-8. They choose their captain for the first round.

3. The first team sends their captain to the front of the class who sits in a chair facing their team, while the teacher stands behind them with the flashcards. Give the team 3 minutes to describe as many words as possible, using only English to the captain who must guess them. The teacher keeps track of how many correct words the team got.

4. Continue to play until all teams have played an equal number of rounds, with different captains for each round.

5. The team with the most points at the end of all the rounds is the winner.

Fill in the Form

Skills: Reading/writing/speaking/listening

Time: 5-20 minutes

Materials: Application form

Filling in forms is an often-overlooked skill for language learners, but life is full of forms. To prepare for this activity, talk to students in advance to find out what kinds of forms they have to fill out in English. Some possibilities include customs and immigration forms when traveling, banking documents, registration paperwork (such as for a doctor or a credit card) and job applications. Whatever students need, a quick Google search should turn up a generic example you can use in class.

Most forms have a fair bit of overlap in terms of requested information, so students should get a quick boost of confidence, but there may be important differences in how dates and addresses are written compared to their first language. Any such variations can be quickly learned, and you can move along to the more challenging sections. The challenges to students will be in the areas of vocabulary used on forms as well as writing responses in the way expected by those who collect the forms.

You can do this as a writing activity, discussing each section with students, or you can complete the forms as a role play. For the role play, make two copies of the blank form so that students working in pairs can take turns playing the "information collector" and the "subject."

Procedure:

1. In advance, find out what kinds of forms students need to fill out in English.
2. Find examples online and print two copies of each form you want to use.
3. Have students take turns playing the parts of the "information collector" and the "subject."

Board Games

Skills: Reading/speaking

Time: 25-40 minutes

Materials: Board game sheet and marker for each student (a coin or eraser)

Board Games often come in the "teacher's resource book" that goes along with the textbook and if this is the case, you're in luck because no prep will be required but you'll have a solid activity that your students will probably love and it has the added bonus of being extremely student-centered. However, don't worry if there isn't a pre-made game in the textbook because it's easier than you might think to make your own. It will only take 5-10 minutes once you get a bit of experience doing it.

Use questions based on the grammar and/or vocabulary that you've been teaching during the previous classes. Have some fun squares, such as, "Switch positions with the person on your right" or, "Go back 5 spaces." The style I typically use is a question of some kind where the student has to speak one or two sentences in response to it. The other students in the group listen for incorrect answers, in which case the student has to move back the number that they "rolled. " You can use dice (which gets loud), two coins (2 heads = 5, 1 head + 1 tail = 3, 2 tails = 1), or a number sheet where students close their eyes and move their pen to choose a number.

Teaching Tips:

Board games have their own lexical set and it may be the first time many students have ever played a board game in English so it's useful to do some pre-teaching. Before you play, you can teach them some key phrases and encourage them to speak only English (it's your turn, go ahead, your roll, pass the dice, let's ask the teacher, etc.).

Dice are my least favorite way to "roll" because they fall off the desk, roll around the room and they can also be very loud. Using coins or a paper sheet with a pen is much more controlled.

If students disagree about whether an answer is correct or incorrect, you can make a joke and tell them not to fight but just to ask you to be the referee. You should think carefully about the game though and make most of the questions easy enough that there are obvious correct answers. If not, class time will be very stressful if you have a big class and many groups demanding attention at the same time.

Before I give the winner of each group a little prize, I'll often make them answer one or two final questions, which I usually take from the game board. It's a good way to review correct vocabulary and/or grammar use with the class in case any group has been off-base but you didn't catch it. A key component of learning language is hearing it and using it again, and again, and again. Help students do this in class by doing quick reviews together at the end of activities.

Procedure:

1. Hand out the "game boards" as well as dice or coins to groups of 3-5 students. Have each student provide their own token—it can be an eraser, a key or a small piece of paper.
2. The students can do rock-scissor-paper to see who goes first. The first student uses the dice or coins to find the number of spaces they will move ahead. That student answers the question and if correct, they stay on that space but if incorrect, they move back the number of spaces that they rolled.
3. The next student rolls the dice and answers a question and so on.
4. The game continues until one student reaches the final square on the game.

Conversation Starters

Skills: Speaking/listening

Time: 10 minutes

Materials: Nothing

Students often struggle with how to start a conversation and this is an activity you can use to help them. It's particularly useful for beginners but it's also possible for advanced level students if you give the students a particular context relevant to them such as "at the water cooler" (business small talk) or "at the drink table" (party small-talk).

The way it works is that you write the beginning of a conversation on the PowerPoint or whiteboard. For example,

A: "How was your weekend?"

B: "It was _____. I _____."

Or,

A: "What did you do last night?"

B: "I _____. "

Or,

A: "Anything interesting happening with you lately?"

B: "Not really, I've just been   . "

Put the student into pairs and they have to engage in a short conversation for about a minute using the starter. If you have adults, you can ring a bell after one minute is up and then they have to quickly find someone else that they haven't talked to yet and start the conversation again. If you have teenagers, it can get a little chaotic to do it that way so I recommend forming two opposing lines. One line stays stationary while the other line moves one person down the line for each round.

Teaching Tips:

An important sub-skill that our students need to be proficient at is initiating a conversation. However, it can sometimes be a bit of a difficult thing even for English native speakers so it's useful to provide our students with opportunities to practice it and also to give them a few set phrases they can keep in their English "tool-kits. " It can be useful to do this activity at regular intervals (every month perhaps) and use different starters each time.

Procedure:

1. Think of a conversation starter. Put it on the PowerPoint or whiteboard.

2. Have students find a partner, either in a line or by themselves.

3. Students have a one minute conversation using the starter.

4. Ring a bell and students have to find a new partner, either by mingling or moving one space down the line to face a new partner.

5. Students have another short one minute conversation. Repeat as many times as desired.

Making Videos

Skills: Speaking

Time: 1-5 hours

Materials: Smartphone and/or computer

For my conversation classes, I rarely give the students written homework. It doesn't make sense and it seems far better to me that my students have to practice speaking. Plus, at least in Korea, everybody loves using their Smartphone so this gives my students another excuse to do this.

I base the homework on whatever I'm teaching. For example, in one of my higher level classes we were talking about good and bad manners, so I had my students choose a specific situation (going to someone's home, at a coffee shop, eating out, etc.) and explain what things you should and shouldn't do. For lower level students, I've done things like telling students to introduce themselves and then giving a few topics that they have to cover such as family, hobbies and hopes for the future.

It's easy for the students to upload the videos on *YouTube* and then send you the link so you can watch and evaluate them. To make it even more fun for the students, I tell them that they can make the video with someone else if they wish. If it's a person in the same class, the requirements are usually slightly higher (for example, five minutes instead of three). But, they could also do it with anybody outside the class. I've had students get their families, little brothers or sisters, girlfriends or boyfriends, international students they know in their dormitory, and even random people on the street to help them. It's usually funny and interesting and it's homework that I truly don't mind grading.

You could show the videos in class if you want, but I often don't since there are always lots of students who are shy (in Korea). However, if students know that other students will be watching their videos, motivation is higher and the videos tend to be better quality. Another thing you can do is to have students watch the other videos and comment on them as part of their homework but be careful with this and make sure to provide specific rules for what kinds of comments are allowed if you teach teenagers because they can sometimes be less than kind.

Teaching Tips:

Getting students to make videos is a particularly effective way to work on functional language or language sub-skills. Some things you could focus on for solo videos include: giving an opinion, offering advice, using more or less formal language depending on the situation, marking the main points of a discourse through emphasis, and verbal cues or transition statements. If there are two or more people, you can focus on the things previously mentioned but could also consider making a request, apologizing, agreeing, disagreeing, asking for an opinion, turn-taking skills, initiating, etc. What you choose to focus on depends on the topic you choose and whether the student is alone or with a partner. For example, in solo speech it can be useful to focus on something like grammatical accuracy, pronunciation or intonation. However, in a pair students could work on offering advice, or transition statements.

Even if you're not stellar at using technology, chances are that students mostly are, especially if they are teenagers or university students so don't let this hinder you. I've found that even the mature students in my classes could figure it out, usually by asking their own teenagers or students (many of them are teachers themselves). Of course, you should put up your own video on *YouTube* first so you at least have a basic idea of the process. If students are having particular problems, I recommend instructing them to Google it in their own language because the question has surely been answered already.

I never give additional points or take away points for things like poor sound or lighting quality as long as I can see and hear them. I instead focus on English use, since it's an English class and not a video making or editing one. That said, if a student uses their creative powers and goes above and beyond what the other students have done, I'll usually give them a bonus point or two and even ask them if I could show their video in class to the other students.

Some students worry about privacy issues so I always mention that I'll grade the videos very quickly (within a day) and as soon as they get an email from me with my comment, they can delete the video. Another option is to have students send you the video itself by email or upload it to a shared *Google Drive* or *DropBox* account.

Procedure:

1. Decide on the criteria for the video: alone/partner/group, length, topic, etc.
2. Explain the criteria very clearly to students and either have them work on it in class or for homework.
3. Students can upload the video to *YouTube* and then send the link to the teacher.
4. There are three options for watching the videos:

– The teacher watches them and writes comments for the students.

– Watch them in class, with an optional Q&A time.

– Students watch each other's videos outside of class and leave a comment. I do not recommend this option for teenagers due to the bullying factor. However, it works quite well with university students and adults.

Bucket List

Skills: Speaking/listening

Time: 10-15 minutes

Materials: None

Optional materials: Example bucket list poster or PPT

Give students about five minutes to create a list of three things they want to do, see, or accomplish before they die. Have them partner up to discuss for 2-3 minutes, then change partners.

Procedure:

1. Begin by asking students if they have heard the term "bucket list." Then, show them an example, or tell them three things you want to do, see, or accomplish before you die.

2. Give students about five minutes to create their own bucket lists.

3. Divide students into partners to share their bucket lists, then have them change partners. Encourage the students to ask each other some follow-up questions about the list.

Describing Something Guessing Game

Skills: Speaking/listening/reading

Time required: 5-10 minutes

Materials: Handout or PowerPoint with approximately 20 pictures

This is a simple warm-up activity that you can use to generate some interest in a topic for intermediate or advanced students or it can also be used as a quick review of the last lesson's contents. For beginners, it's best to play after you've taught them the necessary language to make the sentences instead of as a warm-up at the beginning of class.

Make up a handout or PowerPoint with pictures of around 20 famous people. Give some hints, such as, "He's American," "He's a sport player," and, "He plays golf." By this time the students will have guessed Tiger Woods. You then cross Tiger Woods off their list or delete it from the PowerPoint. Turn it over to the students and they will take turns describing the people to each other.

You can play in pairs, small groups or with the whole class. This activity works for almost any topic (animals/food/clothes, etc.) and is good for teenagers or adults.

Teaching Tips:

A sub-skill that you could focus on using this activity is hedging, which is when we are not sure about something and use language to indicate that. For example, "Maybe it's _____," "It might be _____," "Is it _____?," "It could be _____."

I emphasize that students should speak in full sentences when they are giving hints to their partners. Saying things like, "Man, American, golf" is not useful for helping students improve their English skills beyond the most basic beginners and even then it's questionable. It's useful to put some example sentences on the board such as "She/He has ____ (hair/eyes)." "She/He is from _____." "She/He is a _____ (job)."

As a general rule, the more that you can get students speaking in full sentences, the better off they'll be in terms of language learning. It's far easier to let students just say one or two words, but they're not pushing themselves to incorporate grammar constructions into their speech in a meaningful way. But, of course don't forget that spoken discourse has much shorter sentences than more formal written work, so don't push students to use more complicated grammatical constructions when doing a simple speaking activity like this.

You can put in a few fun pictures to make it more interesting. For example, I'll always include a picture of myself in a situation where it might not look like me because I had a different hairstyle or was wearing glasses. Or, I'll put in a picture of my twin sister (I really do have a twin)! You can also add a picture of a student in the class or another teacher at your school that the students would know.

Procedure:

1. Prepare pictures of famous people on a handout or in a PowerPoint. PowerPoint is easier and better, but check how it will look on the big screen first before using it in class. Sometimes low-quality pictures can look terrible when made bigger. Also, be

careful if you print out the pictures because you'll often need a high quality printer in order to make the pictures easily recognizable.

2. Do one example with the students so they get an idea of how to play.

3. Put the students into partners or small groups. The first student chooses someone secretly and describes him/her to his/her partner, who must guess the person, using hedging if they are unsure about the answer. You can also allow students to ask some "W/H" questions to their partner if they wish.

4. The students switch roles and continue until the time is up. In order to avoid frustration, I usually make a limit for each picture of two minutes because there might be one that the guesser just doesn't know.

Question of the Day

Skills: Speaking/listening

Time: 5 minutes

Materials: None

Ask a question to spark a short student discussion. Current events, new movies, etc. are good topics to get people speaking in English for a few minutes at the beginning of class. If there is a new blockbuster out, that will be of interest to most students. The ones who have seen it can briefly summarize and answer the other students' questions about it.

Procedure:

1. Begin class by asking students how they have been and if anything interesting has been happening lately.

2. Use one of the students' answers as a segue to a current events question, such as, "You saw _____ last weekend? Who else saw that? What happened?" Just pick a movie, sporting event, or other topic that the majority of students are likely to have seen or at least know.

Deserted Island

Skills: Speaking/listening

Time: 5-10 minutes

Materials: None

Deserted Island is an excellent way to uncover what things are most important to students. Tell students that there is a terrible storm and their ship is sinking, but thankfully, they can bring three objects with them. It doesn't need to be realistic or necessary for survival, just something that they want to have with them during their time on the island. Encourage creativity and imagination. Then, have students share their answers with the class (if under ten students), or in small groups (in larger classes), and give a reason why they'd bring each item.

Procedure:

1. Tell students that they are on a ship and it's sinking. Thankfully, there is an island nearby that is already well-stocked with everything they'll need for survival.

2. Each student has to choose three things that they'd like to have with them during their time on the island. It doesn't need to be realistic or necessary for survival.

3. Students share their answers and why they chose each item with the class (if under ten students), or in small groups (in larger classes).

English Central

Skills: Listening/speaking

Time: 10-15 minutes

Materials: Internet connection

    English Central (www.englishcentral.com/videos) is YouTube for language learners. There is premium content and functionality, but you can enjoy many features for free. YouTube, of course, has subtitles on some videos, but English Central takes it to the next level. First, the videos are intended for use with students, so they have been curated and organized by level, topic and/or language skill. Each video is segmented for easy replay of a chunk of speech. Students can also click on a single word to hear it pronounced slowly and learn the definition.

    Pronunciation is one activity you can use English Central for with students. Have them listen to a clip and repeat. You can pause after each phrase or sentence and repeat as needed.

    Begin by playing the entire clip once or twice. Then, replay the clip, bit by bit, for the students to repeat. Each clip is a short story, so you can also watch and discuss and/or summarize it.

Teaching Tips:

    If students have difficulty with a particular word, you can click on that word and it will be played in isolation. If the students have trouble with a sound, rather than a word, there is a pronunciation section that focuses on phonemes.

Procedure:

1. In advance, make sure you will have an Internet connection.
2. Either select a video in advance or let students choose one. There are "courses" that are sets of related videos, that you can work through in a series.
3. Play the clip once or twice first so the students can hear the entire thing.
4. Play one segment at a time and have the students repeat it.
5. End by watching the entire clip one more time and discussing and/or summarizing.

Talking Bag

Skills: Listening/speaking

Time: 5-10 minutes

Materials: Questions cards, bag/box/bowl

This is a simple listening and speaking activity that requires very little in the way of preparation and can be easily recycled from class to class. It's an ideal "time-filler" if you have a few extra minutes at the end of class.

Procedure:

In advance, prepare a bag (or box, bowl, etc) full of question cards (laminate them if you plan to recycle them in other classes).

Variation 1

Draw a question from the bag and read/ write it. Have students ask and answer the question with the person next to them.

Variation 2

Choose one student to draw a question. That student asks the question to one other student, who then draws a question to ask a third student. Before beginning, set a time limit or decide how many students will have a turn.

Variation 3

Divide students into small groups of 3-5. Have one member of each group draw one question to ask, and have each group member take turns answering.

OR

Have each student draw one question to ask their group.

Role-Plays

Skills: Writing/speaking

Time: 20-40 minutes

Materials: Nothing

Give the students a conversation starter to get them going. For example, if you're talking about *feelings* in class that day, you can use:

A: Hey _____, how are you doing?

B: I'm great, how are you?

A: I'm _____ (sad, embarrassed, angry, bored, etc.). ***Anything besides, "I'm fine, thank you, and you?" is good. ****

B: Oh? What's wrong?

A: _____.

B: _____.

Another context that I often use this activity with is *illness or injury*. For example:

A: Hey _____, you don't look (sound) so good! What's wrong?

B: Oh yeah, I'm not good. I _____.

A: Really? _____.

B: _____.

A: _____.

One final context that I use this with is *excuses*. For example:

A: Hey _____, you're _____ minutes late!

B: I'm really sorry. I've been/I had to _____.

A: Hmmm . . . _____.

Give the students about ten minutes to write the conversation with their partner. You can adjust the number of lines and how detailed of a starter you give to suit the ability level of students. For lower level students, it can be helpful to have a word bank on the board relevant to the context so that the writing portion of this activity doesn't get too long (you could also provide them with a detailed, fill in the blank script). Then, the students memorize their conversation (no papers when speaking!), and do a role-play it in front of their classmates if you have a small class of less than ten.

Remember to maximize the amount of time students are talking. With a larger class, there are a few different ways to handle this. You could get pairs to come up to your desk and show you their conversation while the other students are working on something else, you could use it as a speaking test of some kind, each pair could join with one or two other groups and perform for them, or finally you could have students make a video of themselves and send you the link or put it up on *YouTube.*

I like this activity because it's perfect for lower level students who want to practice "conversation" but don't quite have the skills to do this on their own and it's also a good way to force advanced students to use some new grammar or vocabulary that you're teaching.

Teaching Tips:

Having students make conversations is very useful for practicing functional language and speaking sub-skills. I usually choose one or two functions to mention when I'm giving the instructions for the activity and provide a bit of coaching and language input surrounding that, depending on the level—beginners will need more help.

The functions in particular that fit well with partner conversations include agreeing, disagreeing, apologizing, and asking advice. The sub-skills that you can emphasize are things like turn-taking, initiating a conversation, speaking for an appropriate length of time, stress and intonation, responding (really?), and cohesive devices, particularly noun pronoun reference: A: I saw a movie last night. B: Which one did you see? A. I saw Ironman. It was good.

This truly is one of the most useful things you can do in conversation classes, especially for beginner or intermediate students so make sure you try it out at least once or twice over the course of a semester. It gives students a chance to have a real conversation which will build a lot of confidence but they won't have the pressure of coming up with something to say on the spot. That said, it's gets boring if you do this every class; I generally do it about once a month for a class that meets twice a week over the course of a semester.

Procedure:

1. Prepare a conversation starter based on what you are teaching.
2. (Optional) Pre-teach some language that students could use, if you haven't done that already in the lesson.
3. Write the conversation starter on the whiteboard, PowerPoint, or on a handout.
4. 4. Have students complete the conversation in pairs. Then, they must prepare to speak by memorizing and adding in stress and intonation. You could give some individual help to each pair to assist them in knowing what to stress and how to do it.
5. Have students stand up and "perform" their conversation if you have a small class. In larger classes, there are a few other options (see above).
6. Reward teams for interesting conversations, good acting (no reading), and correct grammar/vocabulary that you were teaching that day.

I'm Going on a Picnic

Skills: Listening/speaking

Time: 5-10 minutes

Materials: None

This is an oldie, but a goodie. It gets students talking and thinking critically as well as working on their listening skills in a big way. Students not only have to pay attention objects that people can bring but also ones that they can't in order to find out the rules for themselves.

Think of a rule for items on the picnic, but don't tell the class. For example, "must contain the letter E," or, "must be a countable noun." Tell the students that you are going on a picnic, and give examples of 3-5 items you are taking with you, to give them hints about the rule. Then, elicit from the students what they would take. If their item doesn't fit the rule, tell them they can't take it.

To keep wait times between turns shorter, have large classes work in groups of 2-3, rather than individually. In any case, set a time limit for each person or group making a guess (10-20 seconds, according to their level), or they are out. The group to guess the rule wins.

Note: groups are not out if they suggest an item that doesn't match the rule, or if they guess the wrong rule. The time limit is to keep the game moving, and disqualifying students for not making guesses keeps students from just listening to other guesses to guess the rule without otherwise contributing.

Procedure:

1. Think of a rule for items which can go on the picnic, such as "must contain the letter E," or, "must be countable."

2. Tell the class you are going on a picnic, and give examples of 3-5 items you are taking with you, to give them hints about the rule.

3. Elicit from the students what they would take. If their item doesn't fit the rule, tell them they can't take it.

4. Have large classes work in groups of 2-3, and set a 10-20 second time limit to keep wait times between turns shorter.

5. The group to guess the rule wins.

Give a Reason

Skill: Speaking

Time: 5-10 minutes

Materials: None

To review conjunctions, try out this simple activity. Write some sentence starters on the board using "because." For example:

- I was late for school because _____.

- My mom was angry at my sister because _____.

- I failed the test because _____.

Put students into pairs and they have to think of the most creative reasons they can to finish off the sentences. Compare answers as a class and choose the most interesting ones.

Teaching Tip:

This activity lends itself well to "so" sentences as well that deal with consequences. For example:

- I missed my bus so _____.

- I woke up late so _____.

Procedure:

1. Write some sentences on the board with "because," but leave the reason blank.

2. Put students into pairs and they have to creatively give the reason to finish the sentence.

3. Compare answers as a class.

What Am I?

Skills: Speaking/listening/reading

Time: 10-15 minutes

Materials: Tape or pins and vocabulary words on paper

This is a classic party game that is an excellent way for beginner students to practice asking simple questions. I often use it as a warm-up in the next class if in the previous one we studied about question forms. For more advanced students, you can choose much harder vocabulary words instead of simple ones like you would for beginners. A good topic for advanced students (or a party you are hosting) is famous people.

Write a bunch of animals, jobs, hobbies or whatever vocabulary you want on slips of paper. Then tape or pin one to each student's back so that they can't see what it is. They have to go around to their classmates asking yes/no questions to find out what they are. For example, "Do I have four legs?" After each question, they can make a guess and the other student will answer "yes" or "no." They can only ask each student one question, so they will talk to almost everyone in the class by the end of the activity.

Teaching Tips:

Be sure to pick vocabulary that you are sure everyone is familiar with. This game isn't fun for the student who is unlucky enough to get "armadillo. "

Also, emphasize to students that this game is just for fun and the purpose is to enjoy themselves while practicing some questions in English. While they can just look at their own paper or get someone to tell them the word, it's not useful and it won't feel good to figure out the word through cheating.

Procedure:

1. The teacher prepares slips of paper with the target vocabulary.
2. The teacher pins or tapes one slip to each student's back.
3. Students walk around the class asking one classmate one yes/no question. The classmate answers the question and after each question, they can have one guess as to what the secret thing is.

4. If incorrect, they talk to another classmate and follow the same procedure. If correct, they take a rest, or get another paper from the teacher depending on time. A student can only ask one question to each student in the class—they cannot speak to the same student twice.

Phone Show and Tell

Skills: Speaking/listening

Time: 10-15 minutes

Materials: Students' phones, optional PPT image of a photo from your phone

In small groups, each person chooses one image on their phone to share with the group. They should show the image and discuss what's happening and why they chose to share it.

Teaching Tip:

An easy way to quickly change groups is to number students, for example, 1 to 4. When you change groups, tell all 1's to get together, 2's together and so on. Be sure to show each new group where to sit. If you have ten groups, divide the new groups in half.

Procedure:

1. Optional: in advance, prepare a PPT of an image from your phone.

2. Divide students into groups of 3-5 and ensure that any students who don't have a phone are divided evenly among the groups.

3. Show the PPT and tell students that it is a picture from your phone. Discuss the picture; tell what is happening and why you chose to share that particular picture.

4. Instruct them to take out their own phones and give them 2-3 minutes to choose a photo to share with their group.

5. If you want to extend the activity, you can have students change groups and repeat the activity, either with the same image or after choosing a new one to share.

Draw a Picture, but Someone Else is Talking

Skills: Speaking/listening

Time: 10-15 minutes

Materials: Blank paper

This is a fun way to practice body parts or descriptive words (big, small, long, etc.) and I guarantee that everyone will be laughing throughout this activity. The students sit back to back and one person is the "talker" while the other one is the "drawer. " The person talking describes something that they're looking at to their partner (a face, a body, a city, a monster) and that person draws what they hear. The results are usually hilarious and fun to show to the rest of the class!

Teaching Tips:

Some useful functional language that you can practice with this activity is asking for clarification. You can pre-teach some language surrounding the topic, such as:

How _____ (long, tall, etc.)?

What do you mean?

I didn't understand, could you say it again?

What did you say? I couldn't hear you.

This activity can get quite loud so it's best to ask students to spread out in the classroom, if possible.

If you teach absolute beginners this is also a great activity, but you might have to do it in a more teacher-centered way. For example, the students could describe a picture to you that you draw on the board, or you could describe something to them and they all draw their own versions of it.

Procedure:

1. Two students sit back to back but close enough to talk to each other.

2. Give student A a picture of some kind, based on whatever you are teaching. I usually put something up on the PowerPoint and have the drawer sit with their back towards the screen.

3. Student A describes the picture to student B who must draw it, without looking at the original picture. Student B can ask some questions to student A to clarify if necessary.

4. Compare the original picture with the drawing and laugh a lot!

Line Up

Skills: Listening/speaking

Time: 5-10 minutes

Materials: None

Line up is a quick activity that you can use as an icebreaker, or just about any time for that matter! Students can stand up. Then, give them a criterion by which they have to organize themselves in a straight line. Some examples:

– Oldest to youngest

– Tallest to shortest

– Highest number of people they live with to the fewest

– Number of pets (most to least)

– Birthday month

Students can do this by talking (only in English!).

Teaching Tip:

Be sure to make it clear which side of the line is for which, or it can get pretty chaotic. For example, if you're doing birthday month, be sure to point to the right and say, "January" and then point to the left and say, "December."

Procedure:

1. Students stand up.

2. Give students a criterion by which they must organize themselves into a line. For example: oldest to youngest.

3. Students organize themselves.

4. The teacher can check if students are in the correct place by asking how old each person is along the line.

Is that Sentence Correct?

Skills: Listening/speaking

Time: 5 minutes

Materials: Sentences (can be made on the spot)

This is a sneaky way to get students to make grammatically correct sentences using target vocabulary and also work on their listening skills at the same time. Start off by saying a sentence which may or may not have an incorrect element in it. Depending on the level of the students, you may have to repeat the sentence 1-2 more times.

Elicit some opinions from the students about whether or not they think the sentence you said is correct or not. If incorrect, get the students to tell you why. Continue on with a few more sentences.

It's also possible to do this activity in a bit more student-centred way. In this case, put students into pairs or groups of three. Say a sentence and then get them to talk together about whether or not it's correct and what they'd change about it. Then, elicit some answers from the class once students have already talked about it with their group.

Procedure:

1. Say a sentence that may have an incorrect element in it.

2. Students have to say if the sentence is correct or not.

3. If incorrect, students have to say what's incorrect and what they'd change.

20 Questions

Skills: Speaking/listening

Time: 20 minutes

Materials: Nothing

This is a "20 questions" style game based on whatever you're teaching such as animals or jobs that is particularly effective for working on yes/no question forms and also logical thinking. If you have higher level students, this works well as a warm-up or icebreaker activity. You can leave it open and allow the students to choose any person, place or thing.

The teacher starts the game by thinking of a secret thing and the students can ask the teacher yes/no questions. Keep track of how many questions are asked and incorrect answers count as a guess too. Students can then play the game in small groups or in pairs, which will significantly increase the student talking time.

Teaching Tips:

It is especially important to do a demonstration of this game because in my experience, it isn't played in many parts of the world. You can also coach students a little bit on what good and bad questions types are, such as a guess right at the start of the game is a terrible and too specific type of question but a general question which eliminates a lot of possible answers is a good one (animals: Does it have 4 legs?, or jobs: Do I need to go to university to get it?).

This game is easily adaptable to make it much easier or much more difficult. To make it very difficult, just say that the secret word has to be a noun. If you want to make it less difficult, specify either a person, place or thing. Finally, the easiest version is to choose a more specific category such as animals or jobs. If you choose the easiest version, you might want to reduce the number of questions from 20 down to 10. For absolute beginners, it's useful to write some example questions on the board for them to refer to throughout the activity.

This is another one of those absolutely nothing required in the way of preparation or materials games which can be played with a variety of levels and class sizes (from 1-40). Keep it in your bag of tricks to pull out in case of emergency.

Procedure:

1. The teacher chooses a secret thing for the example. Students ask a yes/no question. The teacher answers the question and puts one tick (checkmark) on the board.

2. Students ask more questions and the game continues until the students either guess the secret thing or they reach 20 questions/guesses. If you have a small class, it's easy to monitor the activity to ensure that each student gets to ask a question. If you have a larger class, you can make a rule that once a student has asked one question, they cannot ask another one until five more questions have been asked. If the students guess the secret thing, they win. If they reach 20 questions without guessing, the teacher is the winner.

3. Each guess also counts as one question, in order to prevent random guessing.

4. Students can play the game in partners or small groups of 3-5. Whoever guesses the correct answer gets to choose the next secret thing.

Random Acts of Kindness Video Treasure Hunt

Skills: Speaking/listening

Time: 1 hour

Materials: one smart phone per group, one checklist of possible acts of kindness per group

This is a scavenger hunt in disguise. Students are given a list of kind acts and they must go out and do as many as they can in the given time. They must also film the kind acts being done.

You will have to tailor the acts you assign according to your situation such as where the school is located and the time available but some easy ones are:

Each group member:

- Write a kind note and leave it on a windshield

- Give a stranger a flower or a hug

- Pick up 3 pieces of litter

- Help a stranger carry something, such as groceries

When time is up, each group should show you the clips they have filmed. If they have an app like Splice, they can stitch the clips together into a single video, but that is optional.

Teaching Tips:

Assign different points for different activities, if some are more difficult to accomplish than others.

I give out extra points for consistently speaking English in the video clips of the tasks being carried out: asking if the person wants a "free hug" or naming the object they are properly disposing of and where they found it, but require each student to speak at least one sentence in English.

If picking up litter is one of the kind acts on your list, it's nice to provide each group with a small bag and some plastic gloves.

Procedure:

1. In advance, prepare a checklist of 10-12 kind acts. Print enough for each group to have one. Include important information, such as the time limit and how much English they must speak in the video.

2. Divide students into groups of 4-5, making sure each group has at least one smart phone which can record videos.

3. Begin by talking about random acts of kindness: are they familiar with the term, have they ever done or received a random act of kindness, etc.

4. Give out the lists and let the class know the time limit and the minimum English they must use in the videos.

5. When time is up, watch the videos and declare a winner: the group who completed the most tasks or got the most points if you assigned different point values.

6. You could extend the task by showing the videos to the class during the next lesson and having them discuss what they did and how they felt.

Running Dictation

Skills: Writing/listening/speaking/reading

Time: 15 minutes

Materials: The "dictation" + some way to attach it to the walls or board.

This is one of my favorite activities which covers reading, writing, listening and speaking. There are a wide variety of English styles you can choose: poems, song lyrics, a short story, famous quotes—the list is almost limitless. For example, you might make up a story or conversation a few sentences long (less than ten). Put each sentence on a strip of paper and you can also put another strip of paper on top to prevent cheating. Put these around the classroom in various locations.

The students will be in teams of two. One person is the reader and one is the writer. The reader gets up and reads a bit of the passage and comes and tells it to the writer. They go back to remember more of it and so on and so on. At the end, the students have to put the song or conversation in order. If you have beginner students, make sure it's obvious enough what the correct order should be. Intermediate and advanced students can handle something with a bit of ambiguity. When they're done, I'll check their writing and if there aren't many mistakes plus the order is correct, that team is the winner. How many mistakes you allow depends on the level of your students.

Tell your students before the activity starts that standing at the strip of paper and then yelling to their partner instead of walking over to them is not allowed or they will be disqualified.

Teaching Tips:

Make sure to let students know what cheating is (yelling, the "reader/speaker" touching the pen, using their phone camera) and if that happens their team will automatically be disqualified.

Make sure to move beyond dictating the sentences down onto the paper into dealing with meaning as well. Require students to put the conversation, song or poem in the correct order. They can write "1, 2, 3, 4" beside each sentence instead of re-writing them.

Procedure:

1. Prepare a simple story or conversation and put each sentence on a strip of paper.
2. Put the papers around the classroom on the wall, equally spaced out.
3. Divide the students into pairs: one writer and one reader.
4. The reader stands up, walks to the station and reads a paper, then goes back to the writer and tells what they read to the writer, who must write it. The reader can go back to a single paper as many times as required.
5. This procedure of reading, speaking, listening, and writing continues until the team has all the sentences down on their paper.
6. The two students put the story or conversation in the correct order.
7. The teacher can check for accuracy and meaning and decide if it's acceptable, or not.

Used Card Salesman

Skills: Speaking/listening

Time: 15-20 minutes

Materials: Playing cards cut into pieces

This is a negotiation activity. In advance, take a deck of playing cards and cut each card into an equal number of pieces (2-4; the more pieces, the longer the game). Mix the cut cards and divide into the number of groups you will have.

Divide the class into groups of 3-5 and give each group their pile of cards. Give them 2-3 minutes to sort their cards and see how many complete cards they can make with the pieces that they have, and which pieces they need to complete their cards. Once the cards have been sorted, instruct them to complete their missing sets. Give them a time limit of about 10 minutes.

The goal is to have the largest number of completed cards at the end. Students will have to negotiate with other groups, trying to get missing pieces while trying to keep all of the pieces they have. You will soon see which group has the slickest salesmen.

Teaching Tips:

With lower level students, begin by reviewing some negotiating language, like how to make a trade. Demonstrate by offering to trade with a student something from your desk, for something on their desk.

You may want to even the odds by having an equal mix of pieces, such as 1-2 complete sets, X number of half sets, and Y number of single pieces. Or you may want to stack the deck, so to speak.

Procedure:

1. In advance, prepare a deck of playing cards by cutting each card into 2-4 pieces.

2. In class, tell the students that they must practice their salesmanship on their classmates. Explain that they will receive cut up cards and must try to make sets of complete cards. At the end of the activity, the group with the most sets will win.

3. Divide the class into groups of 3-5 and give each group an equal share of the mixed card pieces.

4. Allow 2-3 minutes to sort the cards, so each group can see which card pieces they have and make note of which pieces they need to complete a set (a set being a complete card).

5. Give students ten minutes to complete their missing sets, but don't give them any further rules. They should consider as a group whether it would be better to work together or split up and approach different groups at once.

6. When time is up, have each group tally how many complete sets they have and how many single card pieces they still have.

Toilet Paper Icebreaker

Skills: Speaking/listening

Time: 5-10 minutes

Materials: Toilet paper

This is an icebreaker activity for the first day of class so that you can help the students get to know each other in a fun way. Bring in a roll of toilet paper, and depending on the size of your class, tell the students they can take a certain number of pieces (4-7 works well). You can also play this game with a bag of wrapped candies (wrapped for sanitary reasons) and as the student completes each speaking task, they can eat the candy. In fact, maybe all your classes would like this option better but it depends on your budget! Don't give them any other information. Once everyone has their papers, explain that they have to tell the class one thing about themselves for each square of paper they have. For each sentence, they "throw-away" one square until they're done. If you have an extremely large class, you can put the students in groups of 5-6 for this activity instead of playing all together as your would for a smaller class.

Teaching Tip:

Students are always so curious about why they have a choice for how many they chose. Be mysterious and don't give away the secret until everyone has chosen.

Procedure:

1. Divide the students into groups of 5-6 (larger classes), or play together for a smaller class.

2. Students choose the number of pieces of toilet paper that they want depending on your minimum and maximum criteria.

3. Tell the students that for each square they took, they must say one interesting thing about themselves.

4. The first student says one thing about themselves and discards that square into the pile in the middle (or eats the candy!). The other students could make a response of some sort such as "Me too," or "Really?", or "I can't believe it!" The second student says one thing and discards a square. Continue in a circle until all squares are used up.

5. An optional, but fun variation for higher level students is that they can have a chance to ask a follow-up question after each statement, but only one and the fastest person gets to do it. For each follow-up question, they can discard a square into the pile.

Would You Rather

Skills: Speaking/listening

Time: 5-10 minutes

Materials: List of questions

"Would You Rather?" is a fun party game. You can buy ready-made decks, but they aren't ESL specific. I make my own cards, but you can just make a list of questions or do this without materials if you can think of choices on the spot. One example is "Would you rather have eyes like a fly, or eyes like a spider?" The student must choose one and explain why. You can also share your answer and have a short discussion about it.

Procedure:

1. In advance, prepare cards with two choices—the weirder, the better. For example: "Would you rather have eyes like a fly, or eyes like a spider?" If you want to do this without cards, give the student two choices.

2. Have a 1-2 minute discussion. The student can also ask you a question if they would like.

Pass and Ask

Skills: Speaking/listening

Time: 10-20 minutes

Materials: None

Pass and Ask is a simple activity that helps student work on questions and answers. Use any classroom object like a whiteboard marker or pen. Start the game off by holding the marker. Ask a question and then pass it to the person who has to answer it.

There are two variations to this activity. The first one is that the person who answers the question has to ask a question and then pass the marker on. My rule is that it can't be the same question that was just given.

The second variation is that the person who answers the question can pass the marker to someone else who must think of a question.

If you have a class of fewer than ten students, play it all together and there will be enough student talking time. However, for bigger classes, break the class down into smaller groups of 6-10. Circulate around the class monitoring each group.

Procedure:

1. Find a classroom object like a whiteboard marker. Think of a question and ask it to one student. Pass the marker to them and they have to answer it.

2. That student thinks of another question and passes the marker to the person who has to answer it. Or, they pass the marker to someone else who has to ask a question.

3. Continue until everyone has had a chance to play. This is a quick activity that takes

around 30 seconds per student per round. You can play 2-3 rounds if students are having fun with it.

Round Robin Story

Skills: Listening/speaking

Time: 5-10 minutes

Materials: White board, marker (optional)

This activity is easy, low prep, and doesn't require any materials. To begin, have the students sit in a large circle. Start them off with a "Once upon a time _____" sentence. Say it as well as write it on the white board.

The story then builds as it travels around the room. Each student adds one sentence, which you write (with any mistakes corrected) on the board. This is not a memory game—students only need to add a new sentence which continues the story, rather than repeat it from the beginning. It should, however, make sense in the context of the story.

When all students have added a sentence, you can either add a sentence to end it, if necessary, or ask for volunteers to finish the story. Then, the entire class can read the story aloud from the board. If you have not written it on the board, you can retell or summarize it.

Teaching Tips:

For more active participation (and if necessary to prompt/help students), you may want to ask students open-ended questions about the story while it is still being written. Even if they have to refer to the board, the students will be more actively engaged in the story. This should also help each contribution move the story forward, especially if you are getting a lot of descriptive sentences without much plot.

If your class is large, this will take longer than 5-10 minutes, if all students contribute. You could randomly choose students to contribute until time is up, or plan on a longer activity.

Procedure:

1. Have students sit in a large circle, if possible.

2. Begin with a "Once upon a time" sentence. Say it and write it on the white board.

3. Have the student closest to you add a sentence and write it (correctly) on the board.

4. Continue around the room, until everyone has added a sentence or two.

5. Add a sentence to end the story, or have volunteers finish it.

6. Have a student (or several) read the complete story to the class. If you have not written it, summarize or retell it.

Splice Video Introduction

Skills: Speaking/listening

Time: 30+ minutes

Materials: iPhones, iPads, and/or iPod Touches, Splice app, Internet access, large monitor

Splice is a very basic, easy to use video creation app, which unfortunately does not have an Android version, as of writing. Like the QR Code Hunt activity, this is using a bit of technology to make something old new again; in this case, tired old self-introductions.

Begin class by showing a Splice video introducing yourself to the class. The video should be about 30 seconds long. Then, have students work in small groups of 3-5 taking turns filming one another's brief self-introductions of around 30 seconds each. If you are worried about their technological proficiency, there are *YouTube* tutorials which show just how easy it is to use this app. When everyone in the group has been filmed, the videos are stitched together and emailed to the teacher to show on the big screen for the class.

Teaching Tips:

If possible, provide several devices yourself with the app already loaded to save time.

If this is not a first day activity, find out in advance which students have iPhones or iPads and ask them to come with the app already downloaded.

If your class is very large, even 30 second clips will add up, particularly since they need to be filmed, combined, and then shown to the class. So, a shorter alternative might be necessary, such as having students work in groups of 5-6 to create a 20-second group cheer that they create to introduce their group.

Procedure:

1. In advance, prepare a 30-second video using Splice to introduce yourself to the class.

2. Divide students into groups of 3-5 and have them take turns filming one another's brief self-introductions of around 30 seconds each. Larger groups will need more time but fewer devices.

3. Optionally, show a YouTube tutorial, if your students seem unsure of how to use the app.

4. When all students in a group have finished filming, the segments should be stitched together and emailed to the teacher.

5. When all the videos have been emailed and downloaded, show them to the class on the big screen.

Tell Me More

Skills: Speaking/listening

Time: 5-20 minutes

Materials: Topic prompts, phone/voice recorder

This is a test preparation activity for standardized speaking tests. The TOEIC requires test takers to speak on 11 questions for varying lengths of time, while the TOEFL has six questions. Sometimes, preparation time is given but other times it is not. One barrier for many students is that they cannot keep talking, even about a familiar topic. In this activity, you will give your students a prompt and record them speaking, so you can record how long they can speak and how much relevant detail they can give.

Consider for example, the question, "How often do you read the newspaper?" If the answer given is, "Never," the student will get a minimum score because the answer is relevant (as in, he/she answered the question), but the student did not provide any detail. There are many ways this answer can be expanded:

- I never read the newspaper because I am too busy. Anyway, I can hear about important events on the radio as I drive to work.

- I never read the newspaper because I can find out all of the news online or by watching the news on TV.

- I never read the newspaper because I know if something interesting or important happens, I will read about it on Facebook.

Two things have been accomplished in this example: a reason and a detail have been added to the answer. Obviously, the longer the time limit, the more detail(s) should be given.

To do this activity, give students a prompt and record their answer. This will give you the exact length of the student's response and you will be able to review the response to determine specific areas which need improvement. By frequently practicing, the student will become accustomed to the format of the response and can focus on the content of their answers.

Teaching Tips:

Use the materials available from the testing company for the relevant test for this activity.

If you do this with a large class, you may want to have them record their answers and upload them to YouTube or email them to you for homework.

Procedure:

1. In advance, prepare speaking prompts from the relevant test materials.
2. Choose a prompt and have your students work individually to prepare an answer.
3. Record the answer or assign for homework, if the class is large. The completed videos can be uploaded to YouTube or emailed to you.
4. Review the answer with the student for length and completeness of response.
5. Repeat this activity frequently if your students are preparing for a standardized test.

Test Prep: Describing a Photo

Skill: Speaking

Time: 30-40 minutes

Materials: Prepared images and accompanying vocabulary, timer (phone, kitchen timer, etc.) Optional Materials: Recording device

Some standardized tests of English ability have a speaking task that evaluates how well the test taker can describe a picture. The image may or may not be accompanied by vocabulary the test taker must use in his/her description. Therefore, for this activity you should prepare several images and vocabulary, such as a noun and a preposition or adverb.

Depending on the level of the class, you may want to begin with some useful language, such as:

– at the top/bottom

– on the left/right

– in the corner/middle

– "I think/It looks like _____ (is happening.)"

After you have gone over the useful phrases, divide the class into pairs. Have Student A show Student B a picture and ask him/her what is happening. Set the timer for one minute. Encourage the students to describe it in as much detail as possible. Instruct Student A to elicit further elaboration from Student B, if necessary, until it becomes habit to keep talking for the entire allotted time. Depending on the image, you may want to include hints for Student A to refer to:

- How is the weather?

- What else do you see?

- What do you think they are doing?

- How do you think that person is feeling?

Have the students switch roles. You should have a different image for Student A to describe.

Teaching Tips:

Remind the students to speak in present continuous when describing the image. ("The sun is shining. The man is looking at the woman as they walk across the beach. It looks like they are happy.")

If your students have voice recorders or phones, record their responses. This will help them track their progress as well as how long they speak each time.

You can extend the activity into general speaking by having a discussion related to one or more of the photos.

Procedure:

1. In advance, prepare several photos for your student to describe to their partner.

2. Review some useful phrases (see examples above).

3. Show a photo to your student and ask him/her to describe it to you.

4. As needed, encourage your student to continue describing the photo.

Test Prep: Reading Out Loud

Skills: Speaking/reading

Time: 30-40 minutes

Materials: Prepared texts

Optional materials: Recording device

Some standardized tests of English ability have a speaking task that evaluates how fluently the test taker can read a text aloud. To prepare your students for this, choose several short passages for them to read aloud. During class, first model reading the passage aloud and then have your students read it to a partner several times. Walk around the class to monitor and give each student specific pointers after each reading. For example, if his/her intonation or stress needs improvement, mark the text to show which syllables to stress or where the intonation should rise or fall. If your students have voice recorders or phones, have them record your reading as well as his/her final one for review and practice before your next lesson.

Teaching Tip:

I like to use Breaking News English for this activity because there are a number of activities for each story, so you can easily build an entire lesson around one or two passages.

Procedure:

1. In advance, prepare several short passages for your students to read aloud to you.
2. First, model reading the passage aloud, then have your student read it to a partner several times.
3. Monitor, and give specific pointers after each reading.
4. If your students have voice recorders or phones, have them record your reading as well as his/her final one for them to review and practice before your next lesson.

Test Prep Speaking Activity: 5Ws and H

Skills: Speaking/listening

Time: 30-40 minutes

Materials: Prepared speaking prompts, timer (phone, kitchen timer, etc.)

Optional Materials: Recording device

The speaking part of a standardized test of English ability has some similarities with the written essay portion: the test taker is asked to speak with minimal or no preparation time about a topic for a specified length of time. However, speaking tests have other elements as well. For example, some tests have speaking prompts focusing on personal experiences. Some common prompts include:

- Describe a person who has had a great influence on you.

- What is your happiest childhood memory? Why?

- Describe a place you like to visit.

To get full marks, test takers need to give a full answer. To do this, have your students think like journalists: 5Ws and H. To use the above example prompt of an influential person, your students should tell who the person is and how the person influenced him/her. Your students should elaborate by including when and where they met. He/she can emphasize how long they have known each other, why the person was influential, and what specific qualities the person has that impressed the student.

When you think your class is ready, divide them into pairs (Student A and Student B), provide a prompt and set the timer to give them one minute to prepare. When the timer goes off, reset the timer for two minutes and instruct Student A to begin speaking. You may want to record your students' answers, or have them record themselves for the two of you to review and to track their progress.

Procedure:

1. In advance, prepare several speaking prompts for your class to answer.

2. You may want to have an example prompt to model fully answering a question.

3. Whether you model the activity or not, point out that each student will need to expand his/her answer to fill the time. Keeping the 5W and H questions in mind will help him/her remember to include a variety of details.

4. Divide the class into pairs. Give each student a prompt and set the timer for one minute to allow him/her to prepare a response.

5. When the timer goes off, reset it for two minutes and have student A begin speaking. Switch roles and student B can speak.

6. Your students can record their answers if they have a phone or voice recorder.

The Hot Seat

Skills: Speaking/listening

Time: 3-4 minutes/student

Materials: None

This is a great activity if you have a small class of no more than 10 students. Each student has to think of one interesting thing about themselves that they want to share with the class. My examples are that I have an identical twin and that my mom is also one (it's really true!), or that I've been to more than 50 countries. Then one by one, students have a chance to sit in the "hot-seat." They say their interesting statement and the class has to quickly ask five follow-up questions. The best thing about this activity is that there are usually a lot more questions that students want to ask and they'll follow up during the breaks or after class.

Procedure:

1. Each student thinks of one interesting thing about themselves.

2. The first student comes to the front of the class, sits in the "hot-seat," and says their interesting statement.

3. The class has to quickly ask them five follow-up questions, to which the student answers, and then the student goes to sit back down in their regular seat.

4. The next student comes up and the procedure is repeated until all students have been in the "hot-seat."

ESL Speaking Activities for Beginners

Quiz Show Review Game

Skills: Speaking/listening

Time: 30-45 minutes

Materials: PowerPoint chart, or white board and questions

This is a "Jeopardy" style quiz game, which is useful for teenagers all the way up to adults. It works especially well as a review game before a test. Although most teachers spend a lot of time making this game by using PowerPoint, it isn't necessary and it's possible to write up the grid on the whiteboard before class starts in less than a minute. It should only take 5-10 minutes to prepare the questions if you're very familiar with the material so it's a low-prep game.

Make up categories based on whatever you have been teaching. For example: "vocab, can/can't, movies, body, etc." Think of questions that range from easy ($100) to difficult ($500). Put the students in groups of 3-4 and they have to pick their category and question. The students can pick whatever they want, but the key is that if they get it correct, they get the points. If wrong, they get minus that number. I put in a few +/- $500/$1000 and choose your own wager (up to $1000) to make it more interesting and give the lower level teams a chance to catch up.

There are a few different ways that you can get students to answer questions such as being the first entire team to put their hands up, or hit a buzzer but that can get pretty chaotic. Instead, I do this activity in a more controlled fashion with each team choosing questions in order, one at a time.

One very fun category that I like to include is "random," where I ask any sort of question that we didn't specifically talk about in class. It's more like a general knowledge or trivia category.

You could also include a category called, "All about _____" where you ask the students questions about yourself. Only include those things that you've mentioned in class before and observant students will be able to answer.

Teachings Tips:

Something I do to make it more interesting for the other teams who are not answering the question is tell the students that some of the questions from the game are actual questions on the exam that they're usually doing the next week. I don't think I've ever had so many students paying such close attention to anything before! And of course, put in a few of the game questions on the test to reward those who were listening closely.

If you want to make this game more student-centered and also practice writing and questions forms, you can get the students to make the questions. Put the students into groups of 3-4 and give them the general categories. Then, for each category, they have to submit one easy, one medium and one difficult question. Compile their questions and play the game in the next class you have together. A team might be lucky and get their own question, but it shouldn't happen too often.

Procedure:

1. Make a list of review questions. This depends on the number of categories but 25 works well (5x5).
2. Make sure each team gets asked an equal number of questions.
3. Put students into teams of 3-6 and do rock-scissor-paper to see who goes first.
4. The first team chooses a category and a price. Ask them that question. If correct, they get the points and you can eliminate that question from your board. If incorrect, they lose those points and that question remains in play so that another team can answer it.
5. The next team chooses a question. Follow the same procedure as above.
6. Continue the game until most or all of the questions are gone and all the teams have had a chance to answer an equal number of questions.

Q&A

Skills: Speaking/listening/reading/writing

Time: 10 minutes

Materials: None

This is a simple variation on having students make example sentences using their vocabulary list. Students work in pairs of teams, creating a list of WH questions (to avoid yes/no answers) using their vocabulary words. When they have five questions, teams should alternate asking a question to another team and answering the other team's questions.

You can extend the activity with some reported speech practice, which will give teams an incentive to listen to the responses to their questions.

Procedure:

1. Divide students into an even number of teams of 2-4. Then pair two teams together.
2. Give students a few minutes to create five WH questions using their vocabulary words.
3. Have the paired teams alternate asking and answering each other's questions.
4. Optionally, extend the activity by having teams briefly report the other team's answers.

Typhoon

Skills: Listening/speaking

Time: 30 minutes

Materials: White board and questions

This is a fun review game that any age group of students will love that requires a little preparation but no materials. Every single time I play it, my students always want to play again and talk about it for the rest of the semester. Draw a grid on the board, marking one row with numbers and one with letters. 5x5 works well for a 30 minute game. Put in two or three of each of the special letters (T/H/V), secretly on your master paper, but not the board. On the board will just be a blank grid.

54

T = typhoon: lose all your points

H = hurricane: pick 1 team for minus 5 points

V = vacation: get 5 points for free

E = easy question: 1 point

M = medium question: 3 points

D = difficult question: 5 points

Fill in the rest of the grid with these easy, medium and difficult questions. Then depending on how big the class is, make 4-5 teams. They pick a square, (B-6 for example), then you write the letter in the box and ask them the question or reveal the "special square" that corresponds to it. Have a list of easy/medium/hard questions prepared beforehand. If they get the question correct, give them the points and if not, erase the letter in the box and another team can pick that square if they want and get the same question.

Teaching Tips:

If one team is running away with certain victory, adjust it on the fly by switching some squares around but don't be obvious about it. For example, if the team who is in the lead gets a vacation or hurricane, you can easily switch it with an easy question. Then later in the game, hopefully one of the last place teams will get the vacation or hurricane instead (remember a hurricane is where that team can choose another team to lose points, therefore reducing the gap).

To make it more fun, be kind of dramatic when writing the letter up in the grid on the board. For example, just do the single line-stroke to start off T, H, E, etc. and students will be anxious to know what it is (because the horizontal strokes of each letter are missing). I also often say things, "Ooooohhhh, bad weather is coming. " Or, "Hmmmm . . . the sky is getting very dark."

Make sure that all the students get a chance to participate by saying that once a student on a certain team has answered a question, they can't answer again until all the other team members have. However, their teammates can help them by giving some hints if necessary so that the lower level students won't feel embarrassed or like they're letting down their teams.

Procedure:

1. Prepare review questions beforehand, as well as a "grid" with the appropriate letters marked on it (T, H, V, E, M, D).

2. Write the corresponding grid on the whiteboard, but be sure not to reveal the letters. It should just be blank at this point.

3. Put the students into 4-5 teams. They can rock-scissor-paper to decide who goes first. The first team chooses a square and then you reveal which letter it contains. If a special square, perform that action and if a question, ask the appropriate level of question. If the answer is correct, they get the points and that square is finished. If incorrect, nothing happens and that square remains in the game.

4. The next team chooses a square, performs the action, and so on it goes with the next team.

5. Keep track of the total points and continue the game until all squares are revealed.

What's That Called?

Skill: Writing/reading/speaking

Time: 5-10 minutes

Materials: Post-it notes

If you're teaching about classroom vocabulary, then try out this fun activity. Give each student a few Post-It notes and have them walk around the classroom, labelling common objects (clock, chair, textbook, table, etc.). Students will have a pen or pencil in their hand so emphasize that it's walking only and it's not a race to see who can get the most objects!

When you run out of Post-It notes, or most things are labelled, have students sit down. Then, walk around the class and review students' labels to ensure they're correct.

Pick them up as you go and show them to the class. They can say each one.

When you have all the labels, mix them up and redistribute them back to the students who must put the labels on the objects as a kind of review. They can say the word out loud as they do it.

Procedure:

1. Give each student a few Post-It notes. They will take their pencil and walk around the class, labelling the objects.

2. When they're done, check and see if their labels are correct. Collect the papers as you go. Show the paper to the students and ask them to say it out loud.

3. Redistribute the papers back to the students who must put the labels on the objects one more time. They can say the word out loud as they do this.

Basketball Vocabulary Challenge

Skills: Listening/speaking

Time: 10-15 minutes

Materials: Empty trash can, "balls"

This is a fun game that children love! You can play with the entire class if you have fewer than eight students or in teams if you have more, but you need a big space to play it, such as a large classroom with few desks, gymnasium or outside. Place the empty trash can in the middle of the open space. Arrange the students around the room as far from the basket as possible (touching the wall, behind the chalk line, etc.) and give each student a ball. They can be real balls, but I find that a piece of scrunched up scrap paper works best. Then, place a line of flashcards in front of each person leading toward the basket. Five per player works well.

Going in order one student at a time; the students have two choices: aim for the basket, or say the vocabulary word on the flashcard immediately in front of them and move up closer to the basket. If they aim for the basket but miss, they are out of the game and must go sit down. If they say the word correctly, they move up closer and wait until the next round when they have the same decision. If they say the wrong word, they are also out of the game. Continue in a circle until all the players are out of the game, either because they missed a shot, got a shot in the basket or said a vocabulary word incorrectly. You can give a point or small prize to the first player to get a shot in the basket.

An optional variation is to give different points for various shots as you would in a regular basketball game. For example, from flashcards #5/4 = 3 points. Flashcards #3/2 = 2 points. Flashcard #1 = 1 point.

Procedure:

1. Place an empty trash cash in the center of a large playing area.

2. Arrange five flashcards per student leading from the perimeter to the basket.

3. Line students up at the perimeter behind a row of flashcards. Each student has to be holding a ball of some kind.

4. Students take turns in order and have two choices. The first choice is to shoot their ball at the basket. If they miss, they are out of the game. If they make the basket, they get a point. The other choice is to say the word on the flashcard closest to them and if correct, they move up to that location and waits until their next turn. If incorrect, they are out of the game.

5. The winner is the first student(s) to score a basket. Or, if you're giving different points for the various shots, you can play 3-5 rounds and add up the scores from each round.

Only 1 Question

Skills: Listening/speaking

Time: 10-20 minutes

Materials: Pen, paper

Students have to think of one single question about a certain topic. For example, if you're teaching about holidays, they could use any of the following:

"What's your least favorite holiday?"

"What did you do last _____?"

"What do you think about Valentine's Day?"

There are many possibilities but I usually make a couple rules that it must be interesting and also that it can't be a yes/no question. Once students have done this, they ask at least 10 people their question and quickly record their answers with 1 or 2 words. After the time is up, they tabulate the answers and can quickly report to a small group what they found out about the topic. You can ask each small group to share the most interesting thing they learned with the entire class.

Procedure:

1. Give students a topic and have each student make one *interesting* question about it. Give them examples of interesting versus boring questions.

2. Each student talks to 10+ students, using the same question. They quickly write down answers with 1-2 words.

3. Students tabulate the results and report them to a small group of 4-6 people (or the entire class if fewer than 10 students).

Puzzle Finder

Skills: Speaking/listening

Time: 10-15 minutes

Materials: Puzzle pieces (from an actual puzzle or a cut and laminated image)

The objects of this activity are both teamwork (to create the puzzle) and a review of common vocabulary, such as colors, shapes, and common objects. Before class, you should either prepare a puzzle with enough pieces for each student to have one or two each, or print an image which you cut into the correct number of pieces and laminate. The former is easier, but the latter gives you much more flexibility and you can cut the pieces as large as you like.

In order for students to put the puzzle together correctly, they will need to be able to describe their piece to others as they mingle looking for adjacent pieces, as well as listen to others' descriptions.

Teaching Tips:

If using a ready-made puzzle, a child's puzzle will have the right combination of large size and a low number of pieces. If you choose your own image, you can print the pieces even larger, making it easier to work together.

To make the task more challenging, have students describe their pieces to one another, rather than show them. To make the task less challenging, have two puzzles (fewer edgeless pieces) or use an image with obvious elements.

Procedure:

1. In advance, either get a puzzle with enough pieces for each student to have one or two (so, no 500 piece monster puzzles) or print an image (A3 or larger), cut it into the right number of pieces, and laminate it.

2. Give each student a puzzle piece or two, and instruct them to work together to complete the puzzle.

3. According to the level of the students, allow them to show each other the pieces or require them to describe the shape of their piece and the image fragment.

Sentence Substitution Ladder

Skills: Speaking/listening

Time: 5-20 minutes

Materials: Sentences

This is a simple activity to get students to think about how they can use the words they know. They will be very familiar with substitution drills, but this goes one step further to get lower-level students comfortable with using the language a bit more creatively. They have the knowledge, but they may need a push to use it.

Give the class a sentence practicing familiar categories of words (places, activities, etc.) and a familiar grammatical structure. Then, instruct him/her to change one word at a time to make a new sentence. Each position must be changed one time (as in, first word, second word, etc.), but it doesn't have to be done in order. Optionally, you can have them write the new sentences.

An example ladder would be:

Original sentence: I saw a black cat walk under a ladder.

- I saw an orange cat walk under a ladder.

- We saw an orange cat walk under a ladder.

- We saw an orange cat run under a ladder.

- We saw an orange cat run under the bed.

- We saw an orange cat run to the bed.

- We heard an orange cat run to the bed.

- We heard an orange dog run to the bed.

Teaching Tip:

Unless you want to specifically target articles and numbers, you can consider noun phrases as a single unit.

Procedure:

1. In advance, prepare several sentences using familiar categories of words (places, activities, etc.) and a familiar grammatical structure.
2. Have the students change one word at a time to make a new sentence.
3. Each position must be changed one time (as in, first word, second word, etc.), but it doesn't have to be done in order.

Hidden Object Pictures

Skill: Speaking

Time: 10-15+ minutes

Materials: Worksheet, crayons or markers

You may remember hidden object pictures from your childhood. While they may seem a bit juvenile, coloring is currently quite trendy, and your students may get a kick out of this. If you have some Photoshop skills, you could alter an "adult" coloring page to fit this activity.

If you haven't done this before, it is a drawing with a number of objects "hidden" in the picture. Obviously, it is best suited to teaching nouns. Students should work in pairs or small groups, discussing the picture as they look for the list of objects. In any case, you don't want your students to sit silently for an entire class period coloring.

Teaching Tips:

To make sure each person has a fairly equal amount of speaking practice, give each member of the group a part of the list. This will force students to ask each other what objects are on the other lists.

If students color, then you don't need a full set of crayons or markers for each student. Put two complete sets in baskets or cups for each table to share.

Procedure:

1. In advance, prepare a hidden object picture worksheet (there are many available for free online) and, optionally, bring sufficient crayons or markers for the class.

2. Begin with a brief review of the vocabulary related to the hidden items.

3. Divide students into groups of 2-4 and have them work together to find the hidden images.

4. Finish by having students show their pictures and naming the images they have found. You can extend the task by having students describe the main image, as well.

QR Code Hunt

Skills: Speaking/listening

Time: 15-60 minutes

Materials: Internet access, printer, tape/Blu-tack, student phones with QR code reader apps installed

This activity requires a bit more prep than others, but (as of writing) the novelty factor is high enough to draw some students in who might otherwise be too cool for school. Classtools.net makes it easy to put together a QR code hunt, so don't worry if you haven't used QR codes before—if you can type, you can do this activity.

Teaching Tip:

You can go in a few different directions with this activity, and a pub quiz is a light-hearted way to get students talking, just make sure the questions aren't so obscure that your students spend the entire class Googling the answers!

Procedure:

1. In advance, write your questions in a Word document. These can be discussion questions, trivia questions (pub quiz), or you can pre-test student levels, particularly if you are teaching a subject class.

2. Go to http://www.classtools.net/QR/ and copy and paste.

3. Create the QR codes and print.

4. Post the printouts in various places around the class, or better yet, a larger area.

5. Before dividing students into groups, make sure at least one member of each group has a QR code reader on their phone. If not, give them a minute to download an app—there are plenty of them and most adult students will already have one.

6. Divide students into groups of 3-4 and give them a time limit to find and answer all of the questions.

7. Particularly if you plan to assess student levels, as an option you can have students write the questions they find, and their answers.

8. Wrap up the class with a group discussion of the answers.

Last Person Standing

Skills: Listening/speaking

Time: 5-10 minutes

Materials: None

This activities requires students to pay careful attention to each word that's been said in order to not repeat one. It also requires some on the fly thinking and it's fun too!

Choose a topic based on whatever you're teaching. Some examples are jobs, food, animals, things in the kitchen or classroom, etc. Have all the students stand up in a circle. Clap your hands in a beat 1-2-3 and say a word related to that topic. Continue the 1-2-3 rhythm and have the next person in the circle say a different word related to the topic. If students repeat a word, or don't have one, then they must sit down and the game continues with the remaining players. The game finishes when there is one person standing.

Procedure:

1. Have students stand in a circle and assign a topic.

2. Clap your hands in a 1-2-3 beat and say the first word related to the topic.

3. Continue the rhythm and have the next student say a different word related to the topic. If students repeat a word or don't have one, they must sit down.

4. The game continues until there is one person left standing.

My Name is _____ and I like _____

Skills: Speaking/listening

Time: 10 minutes

Materials: Nothing

A way that you can get your students to remember names (and you too!) is to do this simple activity. Go around the class, and have students say, "My name is _____ and I like _____." The next student repeats the previous ones (His name is _____ and he likes _____.) and adds their own. It goes on until it finally gets to you and you can impress the students with your memorization abilities! It works best for small classes of twelve or less. With more than twelve students, divide the students up into groups.

Teaching Tip:

Adapt this to your level of students. For absolute beginners, it might be enough to say their own name and then, "His/Her name is _____. " For more advanced students you could use something like name and what they did last night, or what they ate for lunch for past tense grammar. To challenge them even more you could do something with the future tense, such as next weekend or next vacation.

Procedure:

1. The first student can say the first sentence. "My name is _____ and I like _____. "

2. The second student must repeat the first student's sentence and then add theirs.

3. And so on it goes, until the last student (or teacher) has a turn.

I'm an Alien

Skills: Speaking/listening

Time: 5-15 minutes

Materials: None

I love a no-prep, no-materials activity, and students generally enjoy this one. You begin class by telling the students you are an alien. You landed just a few minutes earlier, right outside the school. Since you are new here, you don't know a lot of words, and you need some help.

You can create a mission scenario, and elicit vocabulary that will help you. Maybe you want to send a letter telling your mother you arrived safely. You can elicit pen, paper, stamp, envelope, post office. Maybe you need to meet someone in another part of the school, such as the cafeteria. You can elicit types of rooms in a school (hall, bathroom, library, etc.) as well as direction words.

Procedure:

1. Begin class by telling the students you are an alien. Since you are new here, you don't know a lot of words, and you need some help.

2. Create a mission scenario, and elicit vocabulary that will help you complete it. For example, you want to send a letter telling your mother you arrived safely. You can elicit pen, paper, stamp, envelop, and post office.

3. You can give a student a chance to be the alien, if you would like to extend the activity.

Word Association

Skills: Reading/writing/listening/speaking

Time: 5 minutes

Materials: Whiteboard and markers or butcher (A3) paper and pens

To introduce a new vocabulary word, write it in the middle of the board or paper and have students take turns adding as many words or images related to that word as possible. For large classes, have students work in groups with separate pieces of paper taped to the wall or the top of the table/grouped desks. After a given amount of time (2-3 minutes, or when you see no one is adding anything new), discuss their answers.

Teaching Tips:

For large classes, butcher paper works best because more students can write at one time. If that isn't possible, have 5-6 board markers available.

If you're using butcher paper (or A3 in a pinch), prepare in advance by taping it to the wall unless students will be working at their desks. If students will be working at their desks, write the word on each table's page in advance, but don't hand them out, until you have given your instructions.

Procedure:

1. Write a single new vocabulary word on the whiteboard or butcher paper.
2. Have students take turns adding as many words or images related to that word as possible.
3. After 2-3 minutes (or less, if no one is adding anything new), discuss their answers.

My World

Skills: Writing/reading/speaking/listening

Time: 10-15 minutes

Materials: Nothing

This is an excellent icebreaker activity that you can do on the first day of class to introduce yourself and then have the students get to know one or two of their classmates. You start by drawing a big circle on the whiteboard with the title, "My World. " Inside the circle there are various words, pictures or numbers that have some meaning to you. For example, inside my circle there might be 1979, blue, 37, a picture of two cats, and a mountain. The students would then have to make some guesses about why these things are special to me. The correct answers are: my birth year, favorite color, number of countries I've been to, my pets, and hiking which is my favorite hobby.

Teaching Tips:

This is a good activity to practice some functional language dealing with correct or incorrect guesses. Teach your students how to say things like, "You're close," "Almost," "You got it," "That's right," "Really? No!"

Remember that the goal of our classes should be to make them more student-centered than teacher-centered, so try to minimize the amount of time that it takes for students to guess what's in your circle. Most of them are quite easy with only one or two more difficult ones. Then, if required, give your students some hints so they are able to get the harder ones. To increase student talking time, it's always better to have students playing this activity with each other instead of only with you.

For beginners, this activity might be a bit of challenge. You could write down these question forms to help them out:

- Is this your _____ (hobby, birth year, age, favorite color)?

- Do you have */a/an _____ (cat, three family members, etc.)?

- Have you _____ (visited, gone to, tried, etc.)?

Procedure:

1. Draw a big circle on the board and write "My World" at the top. Put in some words, pictures or numbers inside the circle that have some meaning to you.

2. Have students guess what each thing means. Give hints if necessary.

3. Students prepare their own "world. "

4. Students can play with a partner or in small groups of 3-4.

Memory Tray

Skill: Speaking

Time: 5-10 minutes

Materials: A tray with several items/PowerPoint/whiteboard and flashcards

Before class, prepare a tray with 10-20 items, depending on the age of the students. Keep it covered while you tell the students they will have a short time to study the tray. Give 20 seconds to a minute, depending on their age and the number of items. If the class is large, a PowerPoint with images, or flashcards on the whiteboard may be better if you can cover and uncover your whiteboard.

When everyone is ready, uncover the items for the allotted time, and then re-cover them. Have students work in pairs or small groups to reconstruct the tray.

Variation 1: Students list the items they saw.

Variation 2: Students need to recall the location of the items in relation to one another.

Teaching Tip:

If you have them come look more closely, remind them to look but not touch, or some competitive students may pocket some items.

Procedure:

1. In advance, prepare a tray of 10-20 items (more for older students) or a PowerPoint with images or flashcards to put on the whiteboard.

2. Divide the class into pairs or small groups and tell them to look carefully at the items.

3. Tell students not to write anything down.

4. Reveal the items for 20-60 seconds, depending on how many items there are.

5. Have the students work with their partners for 2-3 minutes to reconstruct what they saw.

6. The group with the most correct items wins.

Musical Flashcards

Skill: Speaking

Time: 5 minutes

Materials: Flashcards (large enough for the entire class to see), music.

Optional Materials: Timer, second set of flashcards, monitor/overhead projector

Some days, kids are just too antsy to focus especially when the weather is bad and they haven't been able to play at recess. This is good for getting the kids moving around the classroom while still focusing on English.

To set up, have students stand behind their seats with the chair pushed in. Explain to them that as the music plays, they should move in a circle around the class. When the music stops, they stop. You will show them a card. The students must say what it is. If they cannot say it, then they are out and must sit down.

Start the music. Let it play from 5-15 seconds (switch it up each time). Stop the music and quickly show a flashcard. You can go through your deck one at a time and create a discard pile, or you can randomly choose and have some repeats. To make it harder, literally flash the card: show it to the entire class, but for only a few seconds.

Have the students name the flashcard together. If a student doesn't know the word or is too slow to see the flashcard you've shown, then they are out and must sit down.

Variations:

No one gets out, but you need a second set of flashcards. Lay one flashcard on each student desk. Discard any from your deck that are not used. Whoever is in front of that card when you flash it must hold it up and say it. For example, if you hold up a flashcard of an apple, the student standing in front of the desk with the apple flashcard must hold it up and say, "Apple."

For higher-level students, you can have them make a sentence or give the definition, rather than say the word.

Teaching Tips:

Unless your class is very small, your students will probably not have a neat circle to move around. So, before you begin, take them on a practice lap or two with you leading the way. To do this, pick a starting point (desk) and have everyone follow you as you move from desk to desk around the entire class. What is important is that they see which direction to move in and where to go when leaving one group of desks or row and joining another.

If you have a large classroom, your set of flashcards should be large enough for the entire class to see. I use A4 flashcards. Another option is to have PowerPoint slides of each card or an overhead projector. If you make your own flashcards, you are probably making them in PPT anyway. If you've made them in portrait, convert them to landscape. There will be a wide border on the left and right, but the image will still be large enough to see.

To keep things moving, I give a 3-finger countdown and have everyone answer together. This game isn't fun indefinitely, so you want to try to cut several students each round.

Procedure:

1. In advance, prepare a set of flashcards and music.

2. To set up, have students stand behind their seat with their chair pushed in.

3. Explain to them that as they music plays, they should move in a circle around the class. When the music stops, they stop. You will show them a card. The students must say what it is. If they cannot say it, they are out and must sit down.

4. Start the music. Let it play from 5-15 seconds (switch it up each time).

5. Stop the music and quickly hold up a flashcard.

6. If a student can't name the flashcard you've shown, they are out and must sit down.

7. Repeat until there is only one student remaining.

Mystery Box

Skill: Speaking

Time: 5-10 minutes

Materials: Several small objects, a box

I like to use this activity just after teaching adjectives. I'll make sure students have learned words that describe texture as well as the usual size and shape words. This is a fun activity, but it is best with small classes due to the time it takes for each student to have a turn.

Before class, prepare a large shoe box or similar, by cutting a hole slightly larger than fist-sized and covering the hole. Garland or tissue paper work, but a handkerchief is fastest and easiest. Whatever you use, the students should not be able to see inside the box, but they should be able to stick their hand inside.

One by one, have students take turns feeling inside the box. As they feel, ask them questions about the size, shape, texture, etc. Once everyone has had a turn, review the answers students gave while feeling and elicit guesses as to what is in the box. As students guess items correctly, pull them from the box. If no one can guess some items, end by showing them to the class.

Due to the time involved with each child feeling inside the box, this activity is best suited to small classes. You can use anything (not sharp), but children's toys are good for this, as well as letter magnets.

Procedure:

1. In advance, prepare a large shoe box or copy paper box by cutting a hand-sized hole and then covering it with a handkerchief, so students can reach in but can't see inside.

2. Place several small (not sharp!) objects inside. The class should know the names of

the objects.

3. Have students take turns reaching in the box and feeling the objects.

4. As students feel the objects, ask them questions about the size, shape, and texture of the items.

5. When everyone has had a turn, elicit guesses from the students about what they think the objects are.

6. As students correctly identify items, remove them from the box. If the class cannot guess some items, end the activity by showing the remaining items to the class.

Rock-Scissor-Paper

Skills: Reading/speaking/listening

Time: 20 minutes

Materials: Question and answer papers (5 per student)

This is an excellent review activity to do before a test for lower level classes where there are well-defined, closed type questions and answers. On separate papers, make matching questions and answers. Give each student five random papers with a mix of both questions and answers. They have to walk around the class to find their "match. " Once they do, they can rock-scissor-paper and the winner takes both papers and those papers are "out. " In order to increase student talking time, my rule is that students cannot read each other's papers but must find the matching papers only through speaking. If I see students reading, I enforce a penalty of some kind, where I usually take away one of their matches. The students with the most points (matches) after a certain period of time are the winners.

Teaching Tip:

Try to design questions that have unambiguous questions and answers. I mean that each question should have one specific answer and not be possible for others. Do a demonstration with a couple examples before you start so that students understand the game. I'll usually set aside a couple of matches for my demo and arrange it so that two good students get one part, while I keep the corresponding one. Then I "find" the matches.

Procedure:

1. Prepare matching question and answer papers using unambiguous questions and answers. Cut them out into single strips of paper (questions and answers are separate).

2. Give each student five random papers, in a mix of questions and answers.

3. Students walk around the class, finding their "match. " They can do this only by speaking and not by reading each other's papers.

4. Once they find a match, they do rock-scissor-paper.

5. The winner keeps both papers and that set is finished.

6. The winner is the student with the most sets after the allotted time. If there are more than two or three students who are the "winners," you can reduce this by having a final rock-scissor-paper showdown.

7. Check carefully at the end of the game to ensure that papers are indeed matches. It can be a good teachable moment to explain why a potential match is incorrect if a mistake is made.

Tic-Tac-Toe

Skills: Listening/speaking

Time: 15 minutes

Materials: Whiteboard

This is a review game for students to play in small groups. I usually make groups of four and then within the group, there are two opposing teams. Have students make a regular tic-tac-toe board in their notebook or on some scrap paper. Put up a list of review questions in a PowerPoint, or give students a handout. The teams take turns answering the questions and if correct, they get to mark a square on the grid with X or O and the first to get three in a row is the winner. The teacher can act as the referee in case of uncertainty about an answer.

Teaching Tip:

This game isn't fun if your opponent doesn't know how to answer any questions or has never played tic-tac-toe before so in order to prevent this, I put students in teams of two, trying to match a higher level student with a lower level one. Hopefully, at least one of the students will be able to answer questions and has some sort of tic-tac-toe skill. If you know that many students will have a difficult time answering the questions, you can put some answer prompts up on the whiteboard or PowerPoint.

Procedure:

1. Put students in groups of four, two teams of two.
2. Students can make a normal tic-tac-toe board on a piece of paper.
3. Put review questions in a PowerPoint, or give students a handout with them.
4. One person from each team does rock-scissor-paper to determine who will go first.
5. The first team has to answer the first question and if correct, gets to mark the board with either an X or O. The other team answers the next question and gets to mark one spot on the board if correct.
6. The first team to get three X's or O's in a row is the winner.
7. You can play numerous games and even have the "winners" move up and the "losers" move down like in King's court until you have one final team that is the "King."

Steal the Eraser

Skills: Listening/speaking

Time: 10-15 minutes

Materials: 2 chairs, a table or desk, eraser

Divide the students into two teams. Have two desks at the front of the class, facing each other with an eraser in the middle of the two desks. One student from each team comes and sits in the hot seat. Rotate through the class so that all the students get a chance to play at least once. You then ask a question of some sort, which you should prepare beforehand (one round = one question/2 students. Two rounds = one question/student. Include a few extras for a "bonus" round). The first person that grabs the eraser can try to answer the question. A helpful rule is that the student can take the eraser whenever they want, but the teacher stops talking as soon as the eraser is touched. The student then has ten seconds to answer as you count down on your fingers. If correct, they get one point. If not, the other player gets a chance to answer the question after you repeat the full question one more time.

To make it even more exciting or if one team is behind by a lot of points, have a "Bonus Round," where the teams pick their best three players and each question is worth three points.

Teaching Tips:

Emphasize that the first student to touch the eraser must take it in order to prevent any chaos. I also require students to keep their fingers on the edge of their desks when I begin the question. It's important to stop talking the instant one student touches the eraser. If not, students will just grab the eraser and wait for you to finish the question, which is really unfair. It's best to use questions that have very well-defined answers so you don't have to make any judgement calls because half the class will be unhappy with you no matter what decision you make.

Procedure:

1. Prepare two desks facing each at the front of the class, with an eraser in the middle.
2. Divide students into two teams.
3. Each team sends up one person to the front and they sit at the desks. I don't let students choose the person for each round but make them go in the order that they are sitting.
4. The teacher asks a question (prepare the list beforehand), but stops speaking once the eraser is touched. Alternatively, you can have each team appoint a captain who takes turns reading the prepared list of questions in order to increase student talking time.
5. The first player to touch the eraser must answer the question within ten seconds. Count down the time on your fingers.

6. If correct, he/she gets one point and the next two people come up to the front for another question.

7. If incorrect, the teacher reads the question (in full) one more time and the opposing player gets a chance to answer the question within ten seconds.

8. If correct, they get one point. If incorrect, both players sit down and the next pair comes up. You can share the correct answer with the class before saying a new question.

9. Continue until all students have had a chance to play at least once.

What Can I do with a _____?

Skills: Speaking/listening

Time: 5-10 minutes

Materials: An object

Show students some random common object (potatoes are often used for this activity, but I like to use some kind of "trash" to introduce a lesson on recycling.) Have students work as a class or in small groups to brainstorm as many possible uses for the item as possible. Give them a time limit (3-5 minutes), then discuss their answers. If some answers seem too outlandish, have the student or group explain how or why they would use the item in that way.

Procedure:

1. In advance, prepare an object. A potato is commonly used, but it can be anything.

2. Divide students into groups of 3-5.

3. Give them 3-5 minutes to brainstorm creative uses for the object.

4. As a class, briefly discuss their various ideas.

5. You can have the class choose the best idea, if you like.

Daily Schedule Speaking Activity

Skills: Speaking/listening/writing

Time: 10-20 minutes

Materials: Nothing

It seems that in most beginner ESL textbooks there is a unit on daily schedules, such as, "What time do you get up?" or, "What do you do in the afternoon?" A fun activity that you can do is to have students interview their partners. You can pre-select questions for lower level classes or let the students choose their own questions for higher levels. Make sure you specify a minimum number of questions if you let the students choose their own (beginners = 6-8, intermediate = 10+). Have the students jot down a few notes as they go. Then, they have to close their notebooks, and in a group of four, they have to explain their partner's daily schedule to the other pair in their group. The other group can ask a question or two to the person whose schedule was talked about. You can put some example questions on the board to help your beginner students with this.

Teaching Tips:

This is an excellent activity to turn a boring topic into something that's moderately interesting. Being able to talk about daily schedules is quite an important thing for our learners to be able to do, so ignore the temptation to just skip this section when you come to it in your textbook.

I usually give students a set amount of time to interview their partner such as 3 minutes x 2 = 6 minutes. So each person has to ask questions for three entire minutes and then answer questions for the same amount of time. I emphasize that if the three minutes is not up, they can think of another 1-2 questions to ask. After the first three minutes, I'll say, "Stop, change" so that students don't have to keep track of the time themselves (they probably won't).

While reported speech is kind of a higher level concept, you can introduce it briefly in this activity and provide some concrete examples for students to follow. This happens when two teams join together and are reporting what they learned about their partner to the other pair. For example, "Jen said that she _____," or "Tim told me that he _____. "

For beginner level students, you will need to be very explicit about the kinds of questions and answers they could use and make sure they have access to examples of them, either in the textbook or on the whiteboard.

Procedure:

1. Assign the task to the students, specifying if they must ask questions that you've prepared for them, or if they make their own and how many questions. If students write their own questions, it usually takes about two minutes/question for beginners and one minute/question for intermediate level students.

2. Put students in pairs and they can interview their partner about their daily schedule, taking brief notes.

3. Students switch interviewer/interviewee roles.

4. Put each pair with another pair to do the reported speech task.

5. Student A introduces student B to the other pair. The other pair has a chance to ask some follow-up questions.

6. Continue until all four students' daily schedules have been introduced.

Show and Tell

Skills: Speaking/listening

Time: 1-2 minutes per student (no questions). 4-6 minutes per student (with questions)

Materials: Nothing

This is a classic activity from way back in elementary school but it can work well in your ESL classes too. Tell students a few days before the "show and tell" class that they need to bring an object from home that is meaningful to them. If it's something big (a piano) or something that doesn't transport easily (a cat), then they can email you a picture to put up on the screen instead. Students give a short presentation, talking about the item and why it's meaningful to them. The audience can ask a few follow-up questions. In order to make the question time go more smoothly with shy classes, you can put students into teams of 4-6 and each team has to ask one question. You could also award points or a reward to the 3 or 4 students who ask the most thoughtful questions.

Teaching Tips:

This activity is an excellent way to get your students doing presentations in a low pressure way. If they have something familiar to hold on to, they'll feel less nervous than standing in front of the class with nothing. In addition, everybody likes talking about themselves!

Instead of doing this activity in a single class, you could do it over the course of a semester with one or two students going at the beginning or end of class; you can assign specific days to each student.

Procedure:

1. Tell students to bring a meaningful object from home, or send a picture if bringing the object isn't practical.

2. Students introduce the object in a short presentation of 1-2 minutes, depending on the level.

3. The other students listen and can ask some follow-up questions.

Flyswatter

Skills: Listening/reading/speaking

Time: 5-10 minutes

Materials: Whiteboard, 2 flyswatters

This is a game that can energize the class at the end of a long day or semester. It makes an excellent way to review any new vocabulary or as a warm-up at the beginning of the next class. Write the target words on the board in a random fashion. Use 10-20 depending on the age and level of students.

Divide the students into two teams. One person from each team comes up to the whiteboard and each person is given a flyswatter. Give hints to describe one of the words and the first student to hit the word with the flyswatter gets a point for his/her team. If two students go for a word at the same time, the one on the bottom of the flyswatter stack gets the point. If a student makes an incorrect choice, he/she is out (no second chances). I usually start with a very general hint and progress to more specific ones where the answer is quite obvious. It's up to the student whether or not he/she wants to risk it and guess before the answer is apparent to everyone.

To include a speaking element into this activity, I require that student use the word that they slap in a complete sentence to get the point.

Procedure:

1. Divide students into two teams.

2. Write 10-20 vocabulary words on the whiteboard in random fashion.

3. The first two students come to the board and are each given a flyswatter.

4. The teacher gives hints for one of the words, starting with general ones and getting more specific.

5. The student hits the word with his/her flyswatter when he/she knows the answer.

6. The student has to use the word correctly in a complete sentence.

7. If correct, his/her team gets a point and the next two students come to the board. If incorrect, the other student is given a chance to guess the word and the teacher can give more hints if necessary. If both students are incorrect, both will sit down and neither team gets a point.

Can and Should Speaking Activity

Skills: Speaking/listening/writing

Time: 10-20 minutes

Materials: Nothing

There is often a unit in beginner ESL textbooks with "can/can't" for possibility/impossibility and "should/shouldn't" for advice. Here is my fabulously fun way to introduce it, such that even the lowest of the low, quietest of the quiet classes will participate. Tell your students that you want to go on vacation somewhere in _____ (whatever country you teach in) and need their advice. First, do an example with the whole class and then have students work in pairs using the same script (see below). There are lots of different scenarios you can use to expand the activity.

Teaching Tip:

This activity works well for a variety of contexts. With adult students, use something more interesting like, "How can I find a boyfriend?" or "What should I do to be more handsome/beautiful?" To add a degree of difficulty for intermediate level students, have them explain WHY: "You can go to _____ because _____," or, "You can't go to _____ because _____."

Procedure:

1. Do an example with the class. Use this script:

A. Where <u>should</u> I go on vacation this summer (winter)? B. You can go to _____.

Elicit some answers. Students in Korea choose the same places all the time and I usually select Jeju Island, for reasons you'll see later.

A. <u>Should</u> I go in summer? B. Yes, you should. No you shouldn't. Etc.

A. So what <u>can</u> I do there? B. You can _____.

A. How <u>can</u> I get there? <u>Can</u> I go by airplane? <u>Can</u> I swim? B. Hahaha! Crazy teacher. No, you can't.

2. Write the questions and answer sentence-starters on the board.

3. Put students in groups of two. Student A asks questions and student B gives answers (advice) to their partner using these questions.

4. Students switch roles and do it again.

5. Introduce a new scenario such as a businessman or businesswoman visiting from abroad, or a university student from another part of your country coming to visit your city. One student can pretend to be this person while the other one can give some advice about where to go and what they can do.

6. An optional variation of this is to have students prepare their own scenario (or you assign a different one to each group) and a conversation that they will act out in front of the class using can/should for giving advice.

Disappearing Text

Skills: Reading/speaking

Time: 5-10 minutes

Materials: White board, marker, and eraser

This is a good filler activity to practice vocabulary and grammar. Write one (or more) sentences on the board reviewing new material from that class, or from the previous class, if using as a warm up.

This can be done as last man standing or last group/table standing. Begin with all students standing. They read aloud what is written on the board. Remove one word (or phrase) at a time, and have them repeat the entire passage as it was originally written. As students make mistakes, they must sit down and are out. The winner is the student or table which remains standing the longest. If you are using this as a filler you can stretch the game by playing more than one round.

Teaching Tips:

Before you begin, let students know the order of play (table 1, table 2, from left to right, front to back, etc.) to keep things moving along in an orderly fashion. If the game seems too easy, remove more elements at one time (for example, 2 words instead of 1), or in random order. On the other hand, if it seems more difficult than you expected, remove items in order (from beginning to end or end to beginning.)

If you have more than about 15 students, you should have them play in teams, according to your seating arrangement (pairs/ groups/ tables). So, when one person on the team makes a mistake, the entire group is out. This will shorten each round considerably. Since students are less likely to be engaged once they are out, you want to keep things moving.

Procedure:

1. Write a sentence on the white board. Optionally, have a PowerPoint prepared.

2. Have the entire class stand and read aloud what is on the board.

3. Erase one word or phrase at a time and have the class repeat the sentence in its entirety.

4. Anyone who makes an error must sit down, until there is one student, group, or table left standing.

The World Cup

Skills: Speaking/listening

Time: 15 minutes

Materials: A World Cup "draw" and review questions.

First, make up some questions. Review things work well but add in a few random questions to keep it interesting. Then, make up a "draw." You know, the round of sixteen, quarter-finals, semi-finals and the final. If you have an odd number and it doesn't quite work, make up some "last-chance spots" where all the people who lost out in the first round of the draw can compete against each other for the last spot. There are many on the Internet—just search for something like "tournament format." Write up student's names in the draw randomly. To add some more fun and for smaller classes you can get students to pick a country. For bigger classes, wait until the semi-finals before you allow country picking because it will take too long.

Ask the first two students in the draw a question from your list and the person to answer the fastest gets to move onto the next round. Continue until all the rounds are complete. That's it: simple, exciting and fun.

Teaching Tips:

When you are making up the draw, it appears random but it's possible to manipulate it a little bit. Put the top four students in the four separate corners so that hopefully they will meet each other in the semi-final and final rounds in order to make the game more exciting. The best questions are those with one word answers, such as vocabulary. If answers require a full sentence, it will be too hard to judge who the first one to answer is.

Procedure:

1. Prepare review questions; the ones that work best are one-word things like vocabulary or fill in the blank.

2. Make up a "draw" that looks like a World Cup.

3. The first two students in the draw stand up and you ask them a question. For small classes, use the best of three questions.

4. The first student to answer correctly is the winner and moves on to the next round in the draw. The loser is out, unless you have an odd number of students, in which case they'd go into the consolation pool and compete for a chance to get back into the main draw.

5. Continue with the next two students in the draw until you have your eventual winner.

Quiz Circles

Skills: Speaking/listening

Time: 5-15 minutes

Materials: Timer or buzzer, index cards with questions and answers

Optional Materials: Noise control app

This is a spoken review exercise which gets students up and moving in a controlled way that's also heavy on the listening. Try out quiz circles to practice the important listening sub-skills of listening for specific information, and predicting what kinds of questions there will be. Students can also ask what a specific word means if the listener doesn't know, ask the speaker to repeat the question, and ask the speaker to speak more slowly or to repeat a key word slowly.

It's a good alternative to mingling if your students tend to choose the same friends every time you have a mingling activity. This activity can be done sitting if you have movable chairs and the space to put them in circles, but standing is easier.

In advance, you will need to prepare one index card per student with a quiz question and answer written on the same side, so their partner can't read it. Alternatively, you can begin class by giving each student a blank index card and having them create one question and answer. The teacher can monitor for any errors or offer some assistance with this if this option is chosen.

Create the circles by dividing students into two groups. One group will be the outside circle, which will be stationary. The other will be the inside group, which will rotate. If you have an odd number of students, you can either join in or have the extra student join the outside circle and work with a partner. Have the outside circle face inward and space themselves out as much as possible, then have the inside circle stand in the middle facing a student in the outside circle. Let the students know that each time the buzzer rings, the inside group should shift one student to their right.

When you start the timer, each student in the outside circle should ask their partner in the inside circle their question. The inside circle should answer, then ask their own question. If either answers incorrectly, their partner should tell them the correct answer. They should continue moving around until each person has answered each question.

Teaching Tips:

Set the timer according to the level of the students and the difficulty of the specific task. If they are giving definitions to vocabulary words, they will need less time than if they are answering a question about a story you have read in class. Lower level students will also need more thinking time. In any case, keep the maximum time to about a minute to keep things moving.

You may want to let students know when time is half through, so they can switch, or you can have the outside circle ask their questions on the first pass and the inside circles ask theirs on the second pass.

If your class is quite large or the pool of questions low, have two sets of circles. Keeping in mind that literally half of the class will be speaking at any given time, you may want to use a classroom noise control app, especially if there are nearby classes which may be disturbed. The older the students, the more awareness they will have of "inside voices", so some gentle reminders may be all that is necessary to keep things to a dull roar.

Procedure:

1. In advance, prepare one index card per student with a quiz question and answer written on the same side, so their partner can't read it.

2. In class, create the circles by dividing students into two groups.

3. Have the outside circle face inward and space themselves out as much as possible, then have the inside circle stand in the middle facing a student in the outside circle.

4. If you have an odd number of students, you can either join in or have the extra student join the outside circle and work with a partner.

5. Let the students know that each time the buzzer rings, the inside group should shift one student to their right.

6. When you start the timer, each student in the outside circle should ask their partner in the inside circle their question. The inside circle should answer, then ask their own question.

7. If either answers incorrectly, their partner should tell them the correct answer. The teacher can monitor and offer assistance with this as necessary.

8. Continue moving around until each person has answered each question.

Flashcard Sentences

Skills: Speaking

Time: 5-10 Minutes

Materials: Flashcards

Use this for whatever grammar and vocab points you're teaching. Go around the room asking each student or pair a question. Pull a flashcard from your pile and then the student has to make a sentence using the grammar point with that card. A correct sentence gets the card; not correct, and the card goes back at the bottom of the pile. The winner is the person or the team with the most points.

Teaching Tip:

This works best in small classes of eight or less. If you have bigger classes, it's possible to put students in groups of four and have two teams of two competing against each other. You can act as the referee if required.

Procedure:

1. Get a flashcard from your pile.
2. Ask one student or pair to make a sentence with that card.
3. If correct, the student keeps the card.
4. If incorrect, the flashcard goes to the bottom of the pile. Continue until the cards are gone or the time is up.

Me, Too!

Skills: Speaking/listening

Time: 5-10 minutes

Materials: None

This is a simple activity to uncover what your students have in common with one another. If possible, arrange the seats in a circle, so everyone can see each other. Begin by sharing a fact about yourself that you don't think is unique or unusual. For example, "I like to hike in my free time." Any students in the class who also enjoy hiking should stand (or raise their hands) and say, "Me, too!" Go around the circle and have each student share one fact about themselves. You could extend the activity by keeping track of numbers and noting which facts are common to the most number of students.

Teaching Tips:

You may need to remind them that these are not unusual facts; these should be things they expect to have in common with at least one other person.

Procedure:

1. If possible, arrange the seats in a circle.

2. Begin by sharing a fact about yourself that you don't think is unique or unusual. For example, "I like to hike in my free time."

3. Ask any students in the class who also enjoy hiking to stand (or raise their hands) and say, "Me, too!"

4. Go around the circle and have each student share one fact about themselves.

5. Extend the activity by keeping track of numbers and noting which facts are common to the most number of students.

In Front of/Behind/Between

Skills: Listening/speaking

Time: 5-10 Minutes

Materials: Flashcards

Place some flashcards on your board ledge or leaning against the wall at the front of the room. I like to use three sets of three. Place them so that the students can't see the pictures, but show them what is on the flashcards before you place them. Arrange them so that there is one card in front, one in between and one behind. Then, ask some questions such as, "What's in front of the elephant?" or "What's between the giraffe and the gorilla?" The students that can answer the question correctly get a point. I require that students answer the questions in full sentences.

Teaching Tip:

It's easy to adjust the level in this game. To make it easier, reduce the number of flashcards in play. To make it harder, increase the numbers of flashcards and also the variety of questions you ask by including "next to/beside" or "under" and "over/above" if you place some of them in a stack on the table.

Procedure:

1. Place flashcards in three stacks of three on the blackboard ledge or leaning against a wall, so that students can't see the pictures. But, make sure you show the pictures as you are facing them.

2. Choose one student (or a pair) and ask a question. For example, "Where's the elephant?" Students will have to answer, "It's between the monkey and hippo.

3. If correct, the student gets one point.

Chain Spelling

Skills: Speaking/listening

Time: 5 minutes

Materials: Nothing

If you want to practice spelling some vocabulary words that you've been teaching, use this game. Have all the students stand up and the teacher says a word. The first student says the first letter, the next student the next letter, and on and on. If someone makes a mistake, they sit down and you start with the next student and new word. Continue until you have only 1 or 2 students standing. This is an excellent "filler" game if you have a few minutes left-over at the end of class—just use whatever vocabulary you had been teaching that day.

Teaching Tip:

Spelling is an often neglected skill in many classrooms but it's an important one. I now teach academic writing at a major university in South Korea and some students have atrocious spelling which hampers their ability to write well. Nobody will take you seriously, no matter how good your ideas are if you make basic spelling mistakes.

Procedure:

1. All students stand up.

2. The teacher says a word.

3. The first student must say the first letter.

4. The next student must say the second letter, etc.

5. If incorrect, the student has to sit down. The teacher says a new word and the game continues until there are only one or two students remaining.

Bumbling Blindfold

Skills: Speaking/listening

Time: 20 minutes

Materials: Blindfold

If you're teaching about directions (go straight, left, right, turn-around, stop, etc.) this is a fun activity. Blindfold one student and put them at the starting point. The other students have to give them directions so they can get to the finish point without bumping into anything. Be sure to move anything that students could walk into and hurt themselves with. Also caution them that they need to walk slowly and that if they run, they will have to sit down and their turn will be over.

Teaching Tip:

With a larger class, do this in teams to prevent chaos and confusion. For example, divide the class into two or three groups. Each group must choose a captain to go outside and wait. Choose the start and finish point. Bring one captain into the class and only their team is allowed to give them hints. Time them to see how long it takes. Give a penalty (+15 seconds) for not using English. Repeat with the next team and compare results.

Procedure:

1. Have one student wait outside the class for a minute.

2. Show remaining students the start and the finish point.

3. Go outside and blindfold the student and lead him into the classroom.

4. The other students must give him directions to get from the starting to the finish.

Memory Circle Game

Skills: Speaking/listening

Time: 5-10 minutes

Materials: Nothing

This is a game that I often use with smaller classes of less than ten students. To set it up, you need to make a rule about what kind of words or grammar that the students can use. Base it on whatever you are teaching that day in class. For example: animals or past tense. You'll need to adjust the rules and criteria according to the level and age of your students. You want to make it challenging, but not impossible so that everyone can have a chance to play at least once in a round. I'll use past tense for my example.

Everyone will stand up, in a circle, and I will start the game off, "I ate pizza." The next student says, "She ate pizza, and I studied English." The next student says, "She ate pizza, he studied English, and I watched TV." And so on it goes, around the circle. If someone forgets someone or gets it incorrect, they have to sit down and the game is over. I usually let it go until there are 2-3 people left and then I give them a prize of some sort and start over with a new set of criteria.

If you have very low level students, a single word works better. For example, they can say "Cat," "Cat and dog," or "Cat, dog, and fish."

Teaching Tip:

Participate in the game as well to impress students with your memory skills. It's a good way to end the game if it's taking too long—you go and declare the game finished!

Procedure:

1. Assign a topic or grammar point.

2. All the students stand up in a circle.

3. The first student says a word related to the topic.

4. The next student repeats the first word and a new word.

5. The third student repeats the first two words and adds a new one, etc.

6. If a student misses a word, they sit down and are out of the game.

Flyer Time

Skills: Speaking/listening

Time: 10+ minutes

Materials: Prepared flyers/ads and questions

This activity is used to practice answering questions with a visual aid. While your students are unlikely to be asked which bands are playing at X festival, they may need to answer questions about a presentation or report in English. In advance, prepare several event flyers or ads and questions. Prepare some questions that have the answers clearly stated:

– What time will _____ begin?

– Where will this take place?

Also include some questions that require the students to think about the event and use existing knowledge:

– Who do you think will be attending this event?

– Will attendees need to do anything in advance? (For example, make a reservation or buy tickets)

In class, give the flyer to your students and ask them to use it to answer your questions. Explain that not all of the answers are stated explicitly.

Teaching Tip:

The questions should mostly be content questions with a few purpose questions. The more advanced your students are, the more questions you should ask that are not explicitly answered.

Procedure:

1. In advance, prepare several event flyers and questions (see above for examples) for your student to answer using the flyers.

2. Let your students know that not all questions are explicitly answered on the flyer.

3. Have your students use the flyer to answer the questions.

4. Ask the questions. Do not let your students read the answers word for word.

Top 5 Tips for Teaching Low Level Speaking Classes

I get how difficult it can be to teach "conversation" classes to very low level students who can barely say their name or what they ate for dinner last night—we've all been there. Then there are the expectations of the parents, our bosses, and the students themselves that we are supposed to perform a miracle of sorts and turn these very low level students into fluent English speakers who are comfortable conversing in English over the course of a single semester. To make matters worse, we often only see our students for two or three hours a week, if that and in a class or ten or more. It's very unrealistic but unfortunately, it's the situation that we often find ourselves in. Here are a few tips for you.

Don't Hope for Miracles

Just because a boss, the students and parents unrealistically expect miracles from you, doesn't mean that you need to as well. Be gentle with yourself and of course sincerely try to help your students improve their English speaking skills, but in the end it is up to the students to either take what you give them and run with it, or not. If not, there isn't much you can do besides continue to do your best to inspire and motivate. Certainly don't lose any sleep over it. I've had plenty of students in South Korean universities, who, despite having had studied English for ten years or more couldn't even tell me their name or what city they were from. I knew that getting that student to be able to tell me these things by the end of the semester would be a big improvement and that the goal of having an actual conversation was just too far beyond their capabilities that it would have been futile to even try.

When teaching beginners in speaking classes, celebrate the little improvements that you see and focus on those things. For example, the student who struggled with pronouncing a word correctly finally got it. Cherish the moment when a student says something besides, "I'm fine, thank you, and you?" in response to your, "How are you today?" Or the student who had been struggling in a previous lesson but then is able to answer your review question at the beginning of the next class. Enjoy the feeling when one of the very shy students talks to you in the few minutes before class starts. There are plenty of little things in the stages before a "real conversation" that you can celebrate.

Focus on Other Skills First

One of the theories of language learning is that a solid foundation in the more passive skills (listening and reading) comes before the more active production skills (writing and speaking). It's how we learn language as a child; first we listen and then eventually we speak. As we get older, we first learn to read and then we write. Therefore if your students are extremely low level, it can sometimes be unrealistic to focus extensively on speaking if they don't have a solid grasp of reading or listening skills. Even though the class is a "conversation" class, you can slip in some work on these other skills each class and this will help students get ready to speak later. In fact, most of the textbooks in use today introduce the target grammar or vocabulary through a reading or listening exercise. Since it's a "conversation" class, it can be tempting to skip over this and get straight to the speaking part of the lesson, but keep in mind that these things are quite useful for our lower level students for building a solid foundation.

All four skills are intricately connected and can be hard to separate but you don't need to do this. The best classes are often those that delicately balance these four skills and so even in "conversation" or "speaking" classes, don't be afraid to include some of the other three skills as well, although your class should be heavier on the speaking if that is what the students and administration at your school expect of you. Don't forget to think beyond your class and see language learning as a holistic process that happens over years and decades.

In addition, focus on some functional speaking skills, which in some ways are easier to teach and learn than just general speaking because they are so specific and the language is often quite controlled with a very limited range of variations. For example, you could work on giving advice with beginners by teaching them how to use *maybe you could/should* (very polite), *should/shouldn't* (more polite) and *you'd better/you'd better not* (less polite). The level of politeness would depend on the context you've chosen to introduce the language.

Another function that you could easily teach to beginners is apologizing. Something like, "I'm (really) sorry, I _____" is very useful and doesn't require complicated grammar or vocabulary.

Finally, agreeing and disagreeing are also useful and they don't involve complicated grammar. Things like: really, me too, I think so too, ummm how about _____?, etc. are within the grasp of most beginners.

Focus on Vocabulary

One of the main reasons that students cannot converse freely is that they lack the vocabulary to be able to do so. In my experience, this is a far bigger problem for absolute beginners than lack of grammatical knowledge. Think about your own experiences in learning a language—I'm sure you knew what you wanted to say and perhaps even knew the grammar construction that you needed to use but probably just couldn't access that elusive, but necessary word.

If you spend some time each class teaching even a few new words to your students, it will be time well spent. However, be careful not to overwhelm students with too many because then they won't remember anything! I find that the ideal amount is 5 new words per class, which is an amount that anyone can remember quite easily and it's also often possible to maintain these until the next class. Of course, you should review words periodically as well so that they remain in the student's working memory and are more readily accessible to them when needed.

Student-Centered Teaching: Is it Possible?

Student-centered teaching should be the ideal that we all strive for in every single class we teach and it is possible with even a high-beginner class. However, with very low level students it can be extremely difficult to do this and by necessity, you may have to have a more teacher-centered approach. If this is the case, do not worry too much about it, but always be thinking in the back of your mind how you could make each activity more

98

focused on the students and less on you. If there's an activity that is mostly you talking, consider whether or not that's the best activity and think about if there's another one you could replace it with. Remember, it's the students who should be working hard in your classes and not you.

I remember when I did the CELTA course (the 120 hour long ESL teaching certification program from Cambridge University) and how one of my tutors challenged me to make lessons that were more student-centered. I had thought that my lessons were this way already, but I now see that it wasn't true. He challenged me to consider every single thing I did in class where I was at the front of the classroom speaking and whether or not it could be done in a way that had the students either discovering the language for themselves through guided discovery, or using the language in a meaningful way with a partner or small group.

I challenge you to do the same thing that my tutor did for me. Carefully consider every single time you're at the front of the class talking and how you can reduce this talking time and increase the amount of time your students are active and engaged. Sure, it's a harder for them but they'll almost always appreciate it when they see gains in their language skills, which student-centered teaching will bring.

Build Confidence

If students are high school students or adults and have been studying English for years but are still extremely low level, it's highly likely that they have little to no confidence in their English abilities. Remember to meet students where they're at and don't praise only the top students in the class, but also praise the lower levels ones too for any small improvement that they make. Even a simple thing like having a positive attitude towards English that day in class or participating sincerely in a game or activity can be praised. Remember that even a small comment can go a long way towards building confidence and increasing motivation.

ESL Speaking Activities for Intermediate-Advanced

Just a Minute

Skills: Speaking/listening

Time: 5-10 minutes

Materials: Whiteboard, timer

This is a very simple activity that you can use as a fast warm-up at the beginning of class in order to get your students talking. Write a bunch of general categories on the board such as jobs, hobbies, dreams, movies, food, etc. Put the students into groups of 4 and they can number themselves 1-2-3-4. Then, ask one of the students to throw a paper airplane at the board and whatever word it gets closest to is the topic for the first student. All the number ones must talk about that topic for one minute without stopping and if they stop or have a long pause, they've lost the challenge. You can adjust the time limit to be higher or lower depending on the level of students (beginner = 30 seconds, advanced = 2 minutes). Erase the first speaking round word from the board and continue the activity with the remaining three students except that they have different topics. It's helpful if the teacher does an example speech first with a topic that the students choose.

Teaching Tip:

For higher level students, you can require that their teammates listen carefully and each of them has to ask the speaker an *interesting* follow-up question or two.

Procedure:

1. The teacher writes topics on the whiteboard (teacher-supplied, or elicited from students).
2. Put students into groups of 4. They number themselves 1-2-3-4.
3. The teacher does an example speech with a topic that students choose.
4. One student throws a paper airplane at the whiteboard. The topic closest to where it hits is the first one.

100

5. Student one has to talk about that topic for a minute without stopping. The goal is to have minimal pauses and to never stop talking. (Optional: the other three students each ask a follow-up question).

6. Erase the first speaking round word. Another student throws the paper airplane and finds another topic. The number two students talk for a minute. Continue with the third and fourth rounds' students.

Survey Activities

Skills: Speaking/listening/writing/reading

Time: 20-30 minutes

Materials: Survey handout

Give the students a sheet of paper with some questions and they need to find one of their classmates who fit each slot. My general rule is that one question equals around two minutes for intermediate to advanced students so 10 questions would equal a 20 minute activity; it's one minute per question for beginners because they will not be as good at asking follow-up questions. The kinds of questions you could put on your paper include things like: "Do you travel sometimes?" or, "Are you a university student?" Then, if their partner answers yes (encourage students to answer in full sentences!), they write down their partner's name and ask them one (beginner) or two (intermediate to advanced) more questions to elicit some extra information. They can only ask each classmate one question. If their partner's answer is no, they should choose another question to ask them. Prep the activity well before you turn students loose by saying what you're looking for: only speaking English, everybody standing up, talking to everybody in mostly full sentences, writing the answers in English. Get a student to ask you one of the questions first and then ask a student one of the questions so your students have two models of what they need to do. Here is a survey that I would use on the first day of class:

Get to Know Each Other Survey

Name	Do you _____? Are you _____?	Extra Information (W/H _____?)
	from outside this city	
	in third year	
	play sports	
	live alone	
	eat pizza a lot	
	an only child	
	play sports	
	have a part time job	
	have a boyfriend or girlfriend	
	like horror movies	
	in second year	
	take the subway to school	
	think English is the best subject	
	enjoying this class	
	love your school	
	like studying English	

Teaching Tips:

Surveys are perfect for intermediate to advanced students and it's one of the most student-centered activities that I know of.

Surveys are an excellent way for students to practice some important speaking sub-skills, especially responding appropriately based on what their partner tells them. For example, if they are surprised they could respond with, "Really?" If in agreement, they could say, "Yeah, me too. " If in strong disagreement, they could say something like, "Wow! Why do you think that?" You could even put three categories on the board for "Agree," "Disagree" and "Surprise" and elicit a few ideas from the students about appropriate things they could say in response to a statement.

Another important speaking sub-skill is turn taking. I emphasize to my students that there are times when in-depth and lengthy discourses are necessary (a presentation) but doing a survey activity like this mimics small talk. In small talk, the keys are to listen well, ask some interesting questions and follow-up questions, give short, concise answers and not to ramble. I will sometimes give my students an example of a rambling answer and they usually find it funny, but I hope that they get the point too!

Procedure:

1. Prepare the survey, based on whatever you are teaching.

2. Hand out surveys and write up one or two of the question on the board, making it look the same as the handout. Do two example questions with students, one with you asking a student a question and vice-versa for the second one.

3. Students stand up and talk to one classmate asking them one question (any order is okay). If the answer is "yes," they write in the name and ask a follow-up question. They can write one or two words in the appropriate slot based on the answer their partner gave them.

4. If the answer is no, they must ask another question from the survey until they get a "yes."

5. The pair splits up and each student finds a new partner to talk to.

6. The activity continues until the allotted time is finished.

The "Expert" Conversation Activity

Skills: Speaking/listening

Time: 20-30 minutes

Materials: Nothing

Students write down five things that they're an expert in. Once they've written their lists, they circle the three that they think will be most interesting to other students in the class. Next, divide the students up into pairs and give them about 5-6 minutes to ask some questions to their partner about things they are experts in. Keep changing partners for as long as you want the activity to last, but more than 3-4 times gets kind of boring.

Teaching Tips:

This is a particularly useful activity for practicing many of the speaking sub-skills such as initiating a conversation, turn-taking, and appropriate length of responses. You can pre-teach some of these things before you begin the activity. For example, show your students how to initiate a conversation by saying something like, "I see you're interested in _____. What/where/why/when/who/how _____?"

Or you could teach your students about appropriate length of responses by doing one bad example and then one good example. Continue with the bad example by rambling on and on until the students are feeling a little bit uncomfortable and they'll see clearly what you mean.

If possible, try to get students to talk to someone that they don't know. This is particularly helpful for the students who don't know anybody else in the class, or don't have a friend. Having a five minute conversation with someone makes you feel like you know them and these students won't be so alone in future classes. I do this by asking students to choose partners to go with whose names they don't know.

Procedure:

1. Talk about what "expert" means with your students. Tell them five things that you're an expert in.
2. Students make a list of 5 items.
3. Students choose the three things that they think will be most interesting to the others in the class. Tell students to do the same with their own lists.
4. Students find a partner and talk together for 5-6 minutes about the chosen topics. Starting the conversation, turn-taking and changing topics is up to them.
5. Students switch partners and continue.

2 Truths and a Lie

Skills: Writing/listening/speaking

Time: 20-30 minutes

Materials: Nothing

Play in groups of 4-6 in a bigger class, or everyone together in a small class. My general rule is that if you allow minimal or no follow-up questions, it takes around 3-4 minutes per student. However, if you allow 2-3 minutes of questions, it takes about 6-7 minutes per student. It's a good activity to use "always, usually, sometimes, never" or "can, can't" and "I've. " Students write three sentences, one of which is false. They read their sentences and the other students guess the false one. Higher level classes can ask three questions, or question the person for a pre-determined amount of time (2-3 minutes) to determine the false one. A correct guess gets one point. Each student gets a turn to play.

Teaching Tips:

This is a useful activity for practicing the speaking sub-skills of initiating a conversation and responding to something in a questioning way. For example, students will have to say something like, "So you can make/play/do _____? I kind of don't believe you! Tell me _____" if you allow question time.

You can do this as a single activity in one class, or you can also do it over a series of days. For example, I taught at a winter camp where I had the same group of students for 10 days in a row. My class had 20 students, so as a warm-up for each day, 2 students had to go in the "hot-seat" (one at a time) and we got to ask the students questions about their 2 truths and 1 lie for three minutes. I appointed a "captain" to keep track of the points throughout the two weeks. The two winners got a $5 *Starbucks* gift certificate, which was a small way to add some *friendly* competition to the class.

You can also give points to the student in the hot-seat for anyone who doesn't figure out the correct answer. But, either do this or the other way I mentioned above. If you do both, it gets complicated and confusing very quickly!

Emphasize that students must pick things that are "big picture" ideas. The terrible examples I give are things like birthdays, hospital they were born in, name of sister, etc. There is no way to verify this information through asking any sort of interesting questions. Better categories are things like hobbies, travel, part-time jobs, skills and abilities. I have students write down their statements and try to catch any of the bad ones before the game starts.

Procedure:

1. Write three sentences on the board about yourself: two are true and one is not.
2. Explain to students that they are to do the same for themselves.
3. Do your demonstration with one group. Read your sentences and those students can ask three questions (or have two minutes, etc.) to ask questions.
4. Each student in the group must choose for themselves which sentence is false. Reveal the answer and whoever guessed correctly gets a point.
5. The students play the game in small groups, making sure that each person gets a chance to share their three statements. You can help move the activity along by acting as a time-keeper by giving each student's turn a specific time limit.

Problem and Advice

Skills: Reading/writing/speaking

Time: 30-40 minutes

Materials: Nothing

This is an excellent activity for teaching should/shouldn't and better/better not. Write down a problem such as a high school student studying for the University Entrance Exam who is exhausted and can't sleep at night. Have the students prepare some advice for that person in groups of 2-4. When everyone is ready, have the groups share their answers with the class. The most helpful and clear advice gets a prize of some kind; you can either choose the winner or have the class vote on it.

Teaching Tips:

This also makes an excellent homework activity if you get the students to make a video talking about their advice for a certain problem. To make it even more fun, I'll often make my own video of the problem and put it up on *YouTube* for them to watch, either in class or at home. I usually ham it up a bit and add some drama and may perhaps even have a friend make a guest appearance. Students love seeing their teacher on *YouTube*!

Giving some advice or an opinion in a polite way is an important functional skill that students need to learn and this activity is particularly helpful for that. It's worthwhile to spend some time talking about how to make your advice more, or less, polite depending on the circumstance.

Procedure:

1. Think of a problem of some kind, depending on the topic being studied and the level of the students.

2. Ask students to give some advice to that person. Give them time to prepare their presentation in small groups.

3. Each team does a short presentation in front of the class sharing the advice that they came up with. You choose the best, or have the class vote on it.

Story and Questions

Skills: Writing/reading/speaking/listening

Time: 15-30 minutes

Materials: Nothing

Have students write something interesting. Some examples you can use are: most embarrassing moment, scariest thing you've ever done, your dream for the future, etc. Base it on whatever you are teaching in class. Then, distribute the stories to other people In the class. They have to go around the class, finding the person whose story they have by asking questions. Once they find that person, they have to ask three interesting questions about the story.

Teaching Tips:

Emphasize to students that they are to practice asking good *full-sentence* questions. For example, "USA?" is not a good question, while, "Did you study abroad in the USA?" is much better. Also emphasize that students should think of interesting follow-up questions that expand upon their knowledge about that situation. This involves reading carefully so they can avoid asking about things that are already mentioned. You can give your students a couple of minutes before the activity starts to write down a few questions based on the paper they received to help facilitate this.

This activity provides an excellent opportunity for your students to work on reported speech. This is something that high level students are often surprisingly weak at. If you have a small class (less than 10), students can report what they learned about their partner to everyone. If larger, students can tell their seating partner what they learned. For example, students might say something like, "I talked to Min-Ji. She told me that she got in a car accident last year. She said that it was scary, but thankfully nobody got injured seriously. "

Procedure:

1. Have students write an interesting story based on a certain topic. Adjust for length and difficultly depending on your students.

2. Collect stories and redistribute them—one per student, making sure a student does not get their own story.

3. Students go around the class asking people if they have their story. For example, "Did you get in a car accident when you were little?"

4. When they find the person, they must ask them three interesting follow-up questions about it.

5. Do the optional variation of having students tell other people what they learned in order to practice using reported speech.

Find Something in Common

Skills: Speaking/listening

Time: 10-20 minutes

Materials: Nothing

This activity is an excellent way for everyone to get to know each other. The students stand up with a piece of paper and pencil in their hand. They have to talk to everyone in the class to try to find something in common (they are both from Seoul or they both know how to play the piano). Once they find this thing in common, they write it down along with the person's name. Keep going until most of the students have talked to everyone.

Teaching Tips:

This is a great activity for students to practice the sub-skill of initiating a conversation, which is something that many of them find quite difficult. You could coach your students before the activity starts and give them a few phrases or conversation starters to keep in their head if they get stuck. However, since this game is mostly for higher level students, I wouldn't write them on the board because students will be referring back to them throughout the activity when they are capable of remembering a few phrases in their head and can recall them easily.

Many students struggle with speaking because it happens in real time. Unlike in writing, where we can first plan and then produce later, planning and production overlap and often happen at the same time. If our students focus too much on planning, fluency can suffer. If they focus too much on production, accuracy can suffer. In this activity, fluency is far more important than accuracy because the students are having short, small-talk type conversations. I tell my students not too worry too much about choosing the perfect vocabulary word, or exact grammar constructions, but instead just focus on communicating quickly, in a way that is "good enough. "

Tell your students that while it is okay to have short conversations about the thing they have in common, the goal of the activity is to try to talk to most of the people in the class so they need to keep moving and talking to new people. I recommend to my students that they try to spend only 1-2 minutes talking with each person.

Procedure:

1. Students stand up with a pencil and paper in their hands.

2. They talk to another student and try to find something in common by asking some questions. Some kinds of questions that work are things like, "Have you ever _____ (lived abroad)?", "Are you _____ (an only child)?" or, "Do you _____ (have a brother)?"

3. Once they find something in common, they write that down, along with the person's name.

4. Then, they find a new partner and continue until they've talked to everybody in the class or the time is up.

120-90-60 Fluency Activity

Skills: Speaking/listening

Time: 15 minutes

Materials: Nothing

If you want to help your students speak more quickly and fluently, this is the perfect ESL speaking activity for you. Give your students a topic that they know a lot about. For example: good or bad points about their school, university, or hometown. I often give half the students one topic and the other half another just to make it a bit more interesting to listen to. Give your students 3-5 minutes to prepare, depending on their level. But, emphasize that they should just write one or two words for each point, and not full sentences because it is a speaking activity and not a writing one. Then, with a partner, the first student has to give their speech and talk continuously for two minutes, while their partner listens. I use an online stopwatch so that the students can see the clock countdown. Then, I give the students another two minutes and they switch roles.

After that, the students have to find a new partner and the activity repeats, except they have to include ALL the same information as before, just in 90 seconds. Then, switch

110

again, with 60 more seconds. One way to help students make the transition to less time is by giving them 30 seconds between rounds to think about how to say something more concisely, go over in their head the part of their speech where they had to slow down for some reason or to think about where they could use conjunctions.

Give an example of something like this: "I like watching The Simpsons. It's funny. It's interesting. My mother, father, brother and I watch while we're eating dinner almost every night of the week" --->"I like watching The Simpsons because it's funny and interesting. I watch with my family almost every night while eating dinner. "

For lower level students, adjust the times to make them shorter and easier because talking for two minutes can be quite difficult.

Emphasize that students must include all of the key information even though they have less time to say it. Speak more quickly or more concisely!

Teaching Tips:

It can be difficult to find good speaking activities that are focused on fluency instead of accuracy, but this is an excellent one and I try to use it a couple of times per semester.

Emphasize to students that they must include all the same information they included the first time, so they'll either have to say things more concisely or speak faster. Present it as a difficult, but attainable challenge that they can achieve. At the end of the second and third rounds, ask your students how much they were able to include as a percentage. If they did well, tell them to pat themselves on the back for achieving something that wasn't easy. A small motivational moment in your class!

Something to remind students of is that spoken speech is more informal than written discourse, particularly in the areas of sentence length and connectors. When we write, things like "however," "although," and "moreover" are common but in spoken speech we mostly just use simple connectors like "and," "but," and "or. " Also, in spoken discourse the length of an utterance is shorter and we don't need to use complicated grammar.

111

Procedure:

1. Give students a topic and some time to prepare their "speech. "

2. Students give their speech to a partner, talking for two minutes without stopping. Switch roles and the second student gives their speech.

3. Students find a new partner and give their speech again, this time in 90 seconds. Switch roles.

4. Students find a new partner and give their speech again, but in 60 seconds. Switch roles.

Prediction Activity

Skill: Listening

Time: Depends on the listening passage

Materials: Listening passage

This is a simple activity to help students with predicting what they will hear and can be done before any sort of listening exercise. Show students the title or headline of what they'll hear.

For example, the headline of a news story may be, "Tornado Tears Through City." Elicit some questions from the students that they'd expect to hear the answers to.

- How many died/injured?

- Were any houses or buildings destroyed?

- When did it happen?

- Which city?

- How big was the tornado?

– Etc.

This simple prediction activity primes students for what they'll hear. After listening, put students into pairs or small groups and get them to decide if the questions were answered, or not.

Procedure:

1. Show students a news headline from a corresponding listening passage.

2. Ask them to predict what questions they'll find the answers to.

3. Play the listening passage once (or twice if necessary).

4. In pairs, students discuss which of the questions were answered.

5. Discuss answers together as a class.

Cosmo Quiz

Skills: Speaking/listening/reading

Time: 10-20 minutes

Materials: A Cosmo quiz or Cosmo-type quiz

If you are a guy, you may not be familiar with the quiz in each month's edition of *Cosmopolitan* magazine. These generally predict something about your relationship style, finances, etc. In other words, they are quiz-style horoscopes. They are pretty fun to do as a group, because they are not meant to be taken seriously, but can tell you a little something about the quiz-taker.

Prep could not be easier. Find a few old issues of Cosmo and copy the quizzes. Some of them are a bit risqué, so decide for yourself if you want to edit them a bit. I've had all-female classes, and kept it a little racy, but all the students were about my age.

In class, begin with a brief discussion of personality quizzes: has anyone ever taken one, etc. Divide students into pairs or small groups of 3-4 and give them one or two quizzes with the results on a different page. Have them read the questions and discuss the answers, keeping track of their answers, if they want. You can wrap up with a survey of results and questions of how students feel about the quizzes. Are they accurate, fun, or a waste of time?

Teaching Tips:

You can find quizzes on their website: http://www.cosmopolitan.com/content/quizzes/, but the questions are given one at a time, so if you can get your hands on print quizzes, it will make your life easier.

If you think they are inappropriate for your class, you can always just make up a quiz in the same Cosmo style: ten multiple choice personality questions with points assigned to each answer. There are usually results for three point ranges.

You can either give everyone one quiz and each group reads and answers the questions together, or you can have students alternate asking and answering. You can extend the activity by having students change partners and taking a different quiz.

Procedure:

1. In advance, gather several different issues of Cosmo magazine and copy the quizzes. You may need to edit the questions or leave some out.

2. Begin class by asking if anyone has ever taken a personality quiz and how they feel about them.

3. Divide students into pairs or small groups of 3-4 and give them one or two quizzes with the results on a separate page.

4. Have them read the questions and discuss the answers, keeping track of their answers, if they want.

5. Optionally, extend the activity by having groups change partners and take a new quiz.

Travel-Weather-Seasons Task-Based Activity

Skills: Speaking/listening/writing

Time: 30-40 minutes

Materials: Nothing

Almost every ESL textbook has a unit on travel, weather or seasons. Here is an excellent task-based activity that you can do with your students, which will fit into any of these units well.

Put the students into groups of 4-6. The students are a tour company and the customers are my parents who are coming from Canada to Busan (or your city) for a visit. I will show them a picture of my parents and explain about the kinds of things they like and don't like (example: they like walking around, and sightseeing as well as watching sports, but they hate seafood and strenuous exercise). Then, the students have to plan a 1-3 day tour (depending on the time for the activity/level of students) of Busan (or your city) for my parents.

I usually give them around 20-30 minutes for the task, and at the end they have to share their ideas with the class. It's a good idea to think about how many students/group there are, and give a minimum number of itinerary things they should plan and how much speaking time per person is expected. I pick the top groups based upon the following:

1. I think my parents would love the itinerary.

2. They just speak, and don't read from a paper.

3. Their presentation was informative and convincing.

This could also be adapted into a more comprehensive task, such as making a brochure or promotional video or something like that.

Teaching Tips:

Task-based activities such as this one are an excellent way to promote autonomous learning, which is when students figure out the language for themselves. They also promote team-work, which is a valuable life-skill. You can foster these two things by telling your students to see if anyone on the team knows a certain word or grammatical construction first before asking the teacher, and you can also assign some team roles such as leader, note-taker, time-keeper and so on.

I also like task-based activities because they are more of a deep-end approach to speaking where we plunge learners into a task and see how well they cope. This is in contrast to the walk before you run approach where the language is broken down into separate sub-skills. While most textbooks follow this latter method, both are quite useful and we should strive to use a mix of both in our classes.

The sky is the limit for an activity like this and it can be a 25 minute activity or an entire semester. Some ways to make this into a more comprehensive activity would be to have students make brochures or a short *YouTube* video advertising their tour where they have to go to the actual locations. Or, they could write an article to submit for publication to an English language newspaper, magazine or website in your city although that would become more of a writing activity than a speaking one.

This is a particularly good activity if you teach adults who are studying something like hotel, restaurant, tourism or airline services (or they're already working in those fields). You can focus even more on the vocabulary and grammar necessary for this project (and by extension—their jobs too) if this is the case. Even if your students are not studying these things, you can still help them by pre-teaching some vocabulary from lexical groups that they might not be so familiar with in the area of tourism.

Related to this is the idea of appropriateness of register. By this I mean using the appropriate kind of language for the situation. For example, we speak very differently to our sister or brother than we do to a young child or to the CEO of our company. In this case, you can help your students understand what kind of language would be most appropriate for this activity, which is a formal presentation about a kind of informal topic.

Procedure:

1. Choose a task such as preparing a tour for your parents in the city you live in.

2. Discuss expectations including the length of preparation time, length of speech, how many student will speak, what questions to answer, etc.

3. Give students time to prepare and assist if necessary.

4. Listen to their speeches together as a class. Give some feedback to each group and/or ask follow-up questions, or have the students ask follow-up questions.

Chapter Response

Skills: Speaking/writing

Time: 10-15 minutes

Materials: None

Optional materials: Printed list of questions

Chapter endings make handy stopping points to check your students' comprehension and build a bit of interest to keep up motivation for the next chapter. These questions can be answered orally as part of a book discussion or written in a reader response journal and then discussed in class.

Some questions you can ask include:

- What surprised you in this chapter?

- What feelings did you have as you read? What made you feel this way?

- What words, phrases, or situations in the chapter would like to have explained to you?

- Would you recommend this novel to someone else? Why or why not?

- How do the events in this story so far relate to your life?

- Which character do you most relate to? In what way?

- Which character most reminds you of someone in your life? In what way?

- What do you hope to learn about (a character) as you continue reading?

- What do you think will happen next?

- What questions do you have that you hope will be answered in the next chapter?

Procedure:

1. In advance, prepare a printed list of questions about the chapter.

2. Discuss together in class, or have the students write their answers for homework and you can discuss them in the next class.

Character Problems and Solutions

Skills: Speaking/writing

Time: 10-15 minutes

Materials: None

This is a post-reading activity to include in a novel study or use with a short story. Choose a problem a character faced in the story. Discuss the problem and how the character solved it. Then, have your students brainstorm other ways the problem could have been dealt with. This is a sneaky grammar lesson. You can teach modals of regret (could/should/would have done/etc.) without getting too personal with your students.

Teaching Tip:

If your students are lower level, you may want to begin with a complete grammar lesson with scaffolded practice, such as worksheets, for the students to get some more focused practice.

Procedure:

1. Choose a problem a character faced in the story.

2. Discuss the problem and how the character solved it.

3. Have your students brainstorm other ways the problem could have been dealt with.

The Student Becomes the Teacher

Skills: Speaking/listening

Time: 40-60 minutes

Materials: None

Have each student prepare a brief lesson introducing a hobby or interest of theirs. For example, if they enjoy football, they could explain the basic rules. If they insist their only interest is playing computer games, have them introduce their favorite game and explain how it is played. Remind them that they will be explaining their topic to an absolute beginner so they should assume that the other students in the class have no prior knowledge about their topic.

Teaching Tips:

This is not a first-day activity because you need to have an idea of their level and what, if any, scaffolding will be required.

Procedure:

1. In advance, have students prepare a three-minute lesson introducing their hobby or interest. If your class is large or very low level, reduce the time to two minutes.

2. Plan to give each student time to answer questions about their hobby.

3. Depending on the level, you may need to scaffold with a short how-to reading passage, to give them an example of how instructions should be given. As always, model the activity with your own three-minute lesson about your own hobby or interest.

Dictogloss

Skills: Listening/speaking

Time: 10-15 minutes

Materials: A passage to read out to the class that contains numerous instances of the target vocabulary or grammar. A PowerPoint slide with this passage for students to compare their version with.

Put students into pairs. Read out the passage more quickly than normal. Students can take notes with key words. I specifically tell students that it will be impossible to write down every single word but that they should focus on the most important words.

Students can compare with their partners (by speaking). Read out the passage again (quickly) and students again compare. They can quickly write down what they think this passage is. In the end, they can compare their version with the original one.

Teaching tip

See how well students do when they encounter something that is slightly above their level. This can build confidence in a big way and go a long way toward improving listening skills.

This activity can also lead into a lesson on the grammar or vocabulary found in the passage. Or, it makes a nice review.

Procedure:

1. Find or write a passage containing the target grammar or vocabulary (the textbook if often the best low-prep solution)
2. Put students into pairs. Each student needs a pen and piece of paper.
3. Read out the passage quite quickly. Students take notes as they listen.
4. Students compare with their partner, attempting to recreate what they just heard.
5. Read the passage again.
6. Student compare again.
7. Student compare their version with the original one.

Debate This

Skills: Speaking/listening

Time: 5-15 minutes

Materials: None

Think of some controversial statements such as

- Zoos should be banned.

- Smoking should not be allowed inside private homes.

- Junk food should not be sold in schools.

The students can prepare two pieces of paper. One with "agree" and one with "disagree." When the teacher says the controversial statement, each student can hold up the paper that represents their opinion. The teacher can elicit a reason from one or two of the students on each side.

Teaching tip

Be culturally aware for this one to avoid getting into hot water. There are some taboo topics in some cultures.

Procedure:

1. Think of some controversial statements.

2. Show one of the statements to the students. Students can write an agree, and a disagree statement.

3. The teacher says the statement and students hold up the piece of paper that they agree with.

4. The class can discuss their answers.

"Find Someone Who _____" Bingo

Skills: Speaking/listening/writing

Time: 15-30 minutes

Materials: Blank "Bingo" grids or blank paper (optional PowerPoint or white board and marker)

This is a good ice breaker to help students get to know one another or to practice asking and answering questions about likes/dislikes, future plans, hobbies, etc. If I have my own classroom, I keep a stack of blank grids handy but if I'm moving from class to class, I tend to have students use their notebooks.

To save time, I prepare a PowerPoint with possible items to complete the Bingo grid, such as a list of hobbies, jobs, places, etc.—whatever topics you want to include. If I'm using this as an icebreaker, I may list hobbies, musical instruments, school subjects and popular films or games so students may learn that one student plays the cello and another likes to study science. If we are practicing future plans, this list might include jobs, places, types of housing, etc. and students will then practice saying things like, "I want to be a doctor," or, "I want to live in an apartment."

Rather than have a Bingo caller, students must circulate around the class and ask each other questions to mark out items on their grid. For example, if the topic is jobs, they could ask, "What do you want to be?" I have them write the other student's name in the grid, rather than cross it out. So, if a student says, "Doctor," they will write that student's name in that block. Before you begin, give them a target of one line, etc. to get Bingo.

Teaching Tips:

Rather than make a PowerPoint, write the items on the board. To give students more autonomy, give them a topic and have them brainstorm. Have more items than will fit on the grid, but you can use 3X3 or 4X4 grids if you want to make the activity go more quickly.

I encourage students to move around by only allowing each name to be used once per board in a large class. If the class is quite small, two to three times on a 5x5 grid may be necessary. The goal is to have students practicing the target language, rather than standing with one person and saying, "Do you like apples? Oranges? Bananas? Pears? Melons? Bingo!"

Procedure:

1. Optional: prepare Bingo grid cards and a PowerPoint with questions before class. Otherwise, have students use notebook paper. Tell them what size grid to draw: 3x3, 4x4, or 5x5.

2. Have students fill in their grid with items from the PPT or whiteboard, or create their own, according to a given topic, such as hobbies or likes/dislikes.

3. Have students mingle and ask questions to match students to their grid spaces. For example student A asks, "Do you like apples?" If student B answers, "Yes, I do," student A writes their name in the "apples" box and moves to the next student.

4. The first student to get a Bingo by finding different students to complete their grid is the winner.

If I Had a Million Dollars

Skills: Listening/speaking

Time: 10+ minutes

Materials: Nothing; optional AV equipment for song/video

This is an activity you can use to discuss hypothetical situations and to focus on conditionals. Start by playing the Barenaked Ladies song or video of the same name. Then, tell the students that there is a big Lotto drawing coming up and you're thinking about what you'll do if you win.

If you have the students work in pairs or small groups, the activity will be fairly short, although you can lengthen it a bit by announcing to the class some of the more creative ideas you hear—encouraging them to think beyond mansions and luxury cars. To extend the game further, have students regroup themselves every few minutes. At the end, you can ask students to share the best ideas they heard.

To challenge advanced level students, find the song lyrics, cut and paste them into a worksheet, but omit some of the vocabulary words and get students to fill in the blanks as they listen to the song. One out of every 15-20 words works well.

Procedure:

1. Play the Barenaked Ladies song. I used a *YouTube* version with lyrics. Optionally, have students fill in a worksheet with some of the song lyric words omitted.

2. Set up the scenario for students: a big Lotto drawing is coming up and you have a ticket. Give them several ideas of what you would do if you won.

3. Divide students into small groups and discuss what they would do if they won a million dollars.

4. To extend the activity, regroup students every few minutes.

Agony Aunt

Skills: Listening/speaking

Time: 15-30 minutes

Materials: Printed advice column questions and answers, introductory PowerPoint

This activity gets students talking because everyone knows how to solve other people's problems! If the students are a bit more advanced, you can use actual (age-appropriate) advice columns. These can easily be found by searching on the Internet for "teen advice column" etc. The lower the students' level, the more you'll need to grade the language for them, or write your own.

I've done several variations of this activity and it has always been a hit. I begin with a PowerPoint that shows a few advice column letters and answers. Discuss them a bit—most students will be familiar with the concept. Then, give each pair or small group a copy of a letter (not the same one from the PowerPoint).

Version 1:

Everyone receives the same letter. Students are given time to read and discuss the letter and decide the best advice. Then, each pair or group shares their advice with the class. Optionally, the class can then decide whose advice is the best.

Version 2:

Everyone receives a different letter. As above, they are given time to read and discuss the letter and decide the best advice. Then, each pair or group shares their letter and advice with the class.

Version 3:

As in version 2, everyone receives a different letter. As above, they are given time to read and discuss the letter and decide the best advice. Then, they switch letters with another pair/group. Again, at the end, they share their letters and advice with the class, optionally, choosing the best advice.

Version 1 will be the shortest, while version 3 could easily take an entire class period, depending on the number of groups and how many "rounds" you do. I've even incorporated writing and more formal presentation skills by having each group make a poster with one letter and their advice, which they then present to the class. This took two full class periods: one for group or pair work and one for presentations.

Teaching Tip:

I sometimes have students who have never read a newspaper. If they don't seem to understand the concept after several minutes of explanation, I allow an explanation in the first language from a classmate.

If you are familiar with local celebrities popular with your students, you can use current gossip to spice up the lesson. If X pop star has just had a public breakup, write a letter from that person asking for help getting back together or finding a new boyfriend, etc. For the boys, a rumor of a football star being traded works well to get all their advice on how to improve that player's game.

Procedure:

1. Show a PowerPoint with age and level-appropriate advice column letters. Read them together and discuss.

2. Divide students into pairs or small groups.

Version 1:

1. Give each group the same letter (not one from the PowerPoint).

2. Give the groups time to read the letter and come up with some advice.

3. Discuss each group's advice and vote whose advice is best.

Version 2:

126

1. Give each group a different letter.

2. Give the groups time to read their letter and come up with some advice.

3. Have each group share their advice.

Version 3:

1. Give each group a different letter.

2. Give the groups time to read their letter and come up with some advice.

3. Have groups switch letters and repeat.

4. Read each letter and have the different groups share their advice for that person.

5. Discuss each group's advice and vote whose advice is best.

Talk Show

Skills: Speaking/listening

Time: 15 minutes (small class) to entire class period (larger classes)

Materials: Nothing (optional: toy microphones, video clip with monitor)

This is a pair work variation of self-introductions. My higher level students tend to find this more fun than the same old self-introductions they do all the time. I set up the front of the class as a talk show set with a desk and chair (for the host) and a chair for the person being interviewed and divide the students into pairs. Before beginning, I introduce the activity by asking students about talk shows. Most students will be very familiar with the concept. We then discuss what kinds of questions a host might ask.

One pair at a time comes to the front and the two students take turns being the host and the guest. The host is given either a set number of questions to ask or a time limit. After each host's time is up, the teacher can open the floor to "audience" questions.

Teaching Tips:

While introducing the topic, it may be helpful for the students if you write some of the questions they (or you) suggest on the white board for them to refer to as needed. However, you will need to remind them that talk show hosts look at the person as they ask questions.

The larger the class, the less time each pair will have to speak in front of the class. So, if your class is very large, limit each pair to 2-3 questions each before switching roles. If you have a large class and a short period, this may not be a feasible activity for even an entire class period.

Procedure:

1. Before class begins set up a desk and chair and another chair, talk show-style.

2. To demonstrate, find a short clip of a popular celebrity being interviewed on a talk show to show the class, or talk about talk shows: what kinds of questions are asked, etc.

3. Divide students into pairs: interviewer/host and guest. (They will switch roles.)

4. Have one pair at time come to the front of the class (the audience) and hold their interviews. The guests are playing themselves—this is a self-introduction.

5. After a set number of questions (about 5) or your time limit, open the floor to questions from the audience. Then, have students switch roles.

Celebrity Talk Show

Skills: Listening/speaking

Time: 10-15 minutes

Materials: Nothing (optional: toy microphones; video clip with monitor)

This is quite similar to the Talk Show activity above. However, I like to use this at the end of a unit. It's more like a presentation activity, in that not all students will be a celebrity each time the activity is done. Rather, it is spread across the term. This activity helps students think a bit more deeply about the stories they read and connect with the characters.

The "celebrities" are characters from a story we've read, as well as the author. In the talk show format, each is interviewed in turn by a student host, followed by questions from the audience.

Before beginning the activity, it's helpful to discuss what talk shows they've seen, and questions that usually get asked. If possible, show a short clip from a talk show. Have them think about the particular story they have read in order to ask more relevant questions, rather than the same generic questions each time. For example, "How did you feel when _____ happened?" or, "Why did you do _____?"

Teaching Tip:

If you intend to complete this activity throughout the semester, arrange it so the higher level students go first. This way, the lower level students will have more opportunities to learn from the example of others, in addition to the general improvement in their language ability over the semester.

Procedure:

1. Before class, set up a desk and two chairs, talk show-style.

2. To demonstrate, find a short clip of a popular celebrity being interviewed on a talk show to show the class, or explain about talk shows: what kinds of questions are asked, etc.

3. Choose two students to play interviewer/host and guest. You should keep track of who has had a turn, so each student gets to participate over the term.

4. Have the pair come to the front of the class (the audience) and hold their interview. The guests will play a story character or author.

5. After a set number of questions (about 5) or your time limit, open the floor to questions from the audience. Ask your own questions, if the audience doesn't ask many of their own.

Class Memory Quiz

Skills: Speaking/listening

Time: 20-40 minutes

Materials: Nothing

This activity works best for smaller classes of 10 or fewer students because each student will have to take a turn being interviewed one-on-one at the front of the class. Ask each student 2-4 general questions about their favourite food, band, time they go to bed usually, etc. Nothing too personal is best but as to what "too personal" is will depend on your teaching situation.

The rest of the students in the class will have a chance to practice their note-taking skills as they can write down the key points for each answer they hear. Be sure to keep things moving along very quickly so that students don't have the chance to write down each answer word for word. If students aren't that familiar with each other, I always get the student I'm interviewing to state their name before getting started and I tell students to take careful note of this as it will be necessary later.

After interviewing each student, make a quiz for the class. Ask at least one question about each student. For example, "Who loves strawberries?" Each student will have to write down the answer on a piece of paper and the winner is the person with the most correct answers at the end of the activity.

Variation: For advanced students, you might put students into pairs. Student A interviews student B, and takes notes in point form based on their answers. Then they switch roles, and repeat the process. Then, each student could quickly share the facts they learned about their partner with the class before doing the quiz portion of this activity.

Procedure:

1. Interview each student in the class at a fast pace, asking them 2-4 not too personal questions about themselves. Students should take notes as this is happening.

2. Quiz students on the answers to these questions.

3. Check answers and the winner is the person with the most correct answers.

Ask Me About

Skills: Speaking/listening

Time: 10-15 minutes

Materials: Name labels

This is not an activity for students who are very shy. Before class, print sticky name tags with "Ask Me About" and a cheeky prompt. For example: ". . . the first time I got drunk," or ". . . my worst date ever." Have students mingle and ask each other the prompt on their name tags. This is better for adults who know each other a bit and should be used after you've had a few classes together. If you feel that cheeky prompts would offend your students, stick to safer ones such as first jobs, or the best vacation.

Procedure:

1. In advance, print an "Ask Me About" name tag sticker for each student. Each should have a different prompt, such as, ". . . my worst date ever," or ". . . my first job."

2. As students come in to class, give them each a sticker to put on like a name tag.

3. Have students mingle, asking each other the prompts on their tags.

4. Wrap this activity up by asking a few students the best story a classmate told them.

Cocktail Party

Skills: Speaking/listening

Time: 10-20 minutes

Materials: None

Small talk is a necessary skill, but can be difficult for non-native speakers, especially those from countries where such conversation is not common. Explain to the students that they are at a cocktail party being thrown by their spouse/partner's company. They must engage in small talk with a group of 3-4 people for 2-3 minutes. You may need to scaffold the activity with common cocktail party conversation: current events, sports, even the weather, if they must. Let them know certain topics are typically NOT appropriate at a cocktail party: political opinions, religious discussions, salary, or any other controversial topics. Additionally, demonstrate how to ask follow-up questions.

The main points of the activity are to practice speaking with relative strangers about inconsequential topics and asking follow-up questions. Wrap up the activity by asking each group what topics they discussed and give feedback.

Teaching Tip:

Depending on the level of your students, when you demonstrate the activity, you may need to bring to their attention that you are making follow-up questions based on your partner's answers. Otherwise, your students may end up asking each other a list of unrelated questions without listening to the answers.

132

Procedure:

1. Explain to the class that they will be attending a cocktail party for their spouse/partner's company. Their spouse/partner is called away from them (to answer a call, talk to the boss, whatever), so they must mingle alone.

2. Elicit from students typical topics of cocktail party conversation. Add to the list, as necessary: current events, sports, favorite TV shows (particularly very popular ones that the other guests are likely to be familiar with), etc.

3. Elicit from students topics of conversation which would NOT be appropriate, such as salary, age, religion, etc. If necessary, explain that these topics would be considered too personal or controversial for a cocktail party.

4. Have students stand and begin to mingle.

5. After 2-3 minutes, have students change groups. Time allowing, have them chat in three groups for 2-3 minutes each.

Excuse Me, What did You Say?

Skills: Speaking/listening

Time: 10-15 minutes

Materials: Listening passage

It's often the case that we have to infer meaning from something, even though we didn't understand 100% of the words spoken. It may be a noisy restaurant or bar, the person is speaking very quietly, or for any other reason. This activity helps our students out with this skill.

Tell students that you're going to read something to them but that you've been teaching all day and your voice is tired or weak. Or, use a different accent or speak very quickly. Whatever the case, make sure that not all the words can be understood easily. Students can jot down some notes as this is happening with key words.

After reading the passage, in pairs, students have to try to figure out the main ideas even though they didn't understand everything. You may also allow the students to ask some clarification questions.

Procedure:

1. Choose a listening passage to read out loud.

2. Read it in a way that's a little bit difficult to understand (too fast, tired or weak voice, etc.).

3. Students jot down the key words they hear and discuss the main ideas with a partner.

4. Discuss the main idea together as a class.

5. Read the passage again in a more easily understood voice.

Complaint Desk

Skills: Speaking/listening

Time: 10+ minutes

Materials: None

Complaining, apologizing, and customer service vary from country to country, so your students may not know how to complain in English. In this role play, students will take turns complaining to a customer service desk and being the representative dealing with the complaints. You can give them a scenario, including the type of business and reason for the complaint, or you can have them brainstorm their own.

Begin the lesson with some useful vocabulary, such as:

– Excuse me,

– I'm sorry, but…

– Would you mind…?

– How can I help?

– What exactly is the problem?

– I'm terribly/so sorry (to hear that.)

- To make up for this…

Then, divide your students into pairs. If you are not giving them a scenario, give them 2-3 minutes to brainstorm a time when they had a customer service complaint. You may want to make some suggestions, such as defective merchandise, a disappointing meal, or an incorrect bill. Have the pairs then take turns being the customer and being the employee.

Teaching Tip:

The higher the level of the class, encourage students to use a bit more creativity: try to negotiate a lower bill, or (as customer service) give reasons to deny their request, for example.

Procedure:

1. Begin class with an introduction on complaining and apologizing in English and useful vocabulary for making a complaint to customer service.
2. Divide students into pairs. Give them a scenario, or 2-3 minutes to brainstorm their own.
3. Have students take turns being the customer and the customer service representative.

Vocabulary Apples to Apples

Skills: Listening/speaking

Time: 30+ minutes, including deck-building

Materials: Paper, pen/pencils, textbooks, and scissors

Apples to Apples is a game in which players defend their choice of card played. This version is somewhat different than the actual Apples to Apples game, in order to increase speaking time. Before playing, students need to make two decks of cards using vocabulary words. This is best done at the end of a semester or book, so that there are more words to play with. You may also want to encourage them to brainstorm words they've learned previously.

For deck-building, divide the students into at least two groups: nouns and adjectives. If you have a large class, you may wish to further divide them, for example, into person, place and thing groups. The groups should compile as many nouns and adjectives as they can. To keep the two decks easily identifiable, you may wish to use two colors of paper or blank and ruled paper, which has been cut into 8-10 pieces.

When the groups have finished creating their cards, collect them, keeping the nouns and adjectives separate. Divide the class into groups of 5-8 students and have each group pick a judge. This person will be in charge of the decks of cards and also will have to choose the winner of each round. Each judge should be given an equal share of the two decks.

Have one group help you play a demonstration round in which you are the judge. Deal each group member five noun cards. Turn over one adjective card and have each student choose the noun card in their hand that best matches the adjective and give it to you. Read each of their cards and have them explain why their word is the best match. When all students have spoken, announce which card is the winner, and why.

Have the judge in each group deal five noun cards to their groups and turn over/display one adjective card per round. Each player must choose the noun card in their hand which they feel best matches that adjective and give it to the judge. The judge takes all of the noun cards and shows each card one at a time. Each player must defend their card when the judge shows it.

Example:

If the judge draws the word *big*, the other students may submit nouns like *watermelon*, *elephant*, *heart*, and *day*. The students could then defend their choices with a single sentence:

A: A watermelon is a big fruit.

B: An elephant is a big animal.

136

C: A kind person has a big heart.

D: An important day is a big one.

The students should then be encouraged to keep talking in order to convince the judge that their answer is the best.

When all players have spoken, the judge will decide the winner of that round. Each player will be given one more noun card by the judge. The judge will then give both decks to the winner of the round who becomes the new judge. He/she turns over the next adjective card to start the next round. If there are not many cards (vocabulary words) to play with, you may want to mix the discards back in to the live decks.

Teaching Tip:

While you can save a fair bit of class time by preparing the decks yourself, you can sneak in a bit of parts of speech review for students if they have to make the cards themselves. Additionally, as they are compiling the decks, students are also likely to come across words they have forgotten. This gives them a chance to discuss vocab with their teammates before the game begins (at which point their teammates will have little incentive to help.)

Procedure:

1. Before class, prepare cards by cutting sheets of colored printer paper into 8-10 pieces. Two different colors should be used.

2. Divide students into groups to build two decks of cards: nouns and adjectives. Students should use their textbooks and also brainstorm as many words as they can and write one word per card.

3. When the decks are ready, divide the students into groups of 5-8.

4. Divide the two decks equally between the groups, keeping the two separate.

5. Have one group come to the front of the class to demonstrate. You will be the judge.

6. Turn over one adjective card. Have your group look at their cards, choose the noun that best matches the adjective, and give it to you.

7. Read each noun card and the student who gave it to you must defend their choice (see example above). Choose the best answer and tell the class why.

8. Have each group play rock-scissor-paper to choose the first judge for their group and play one round.

9. After each round, each player is dealt a new noun card, and the winner becomes the new judge (or you can have them rotate in a circle.)

10. Used cards can be mixed back into the decks if there aren't many cards.

Take Sides

Skills: Speaking/listening

Time: 15+ minutes

Materials: None

This is a debate topic which may be controversial, depending on where you are teaching, but it is something most people have an opinion about. Divide your class into two teams: environmentalists and oil people.

Give them the following scenario: oil has been found in your region, but in an area which has not been developed and many people enjoy visiting due to its unspoiled beauty. The proposed project to extract the oil would bring jobs and money to the area, but would spoil the beauty of the area and interfere with the habitat of local wildlife. The oil people are holding a town hall meeting to address the concerns of the environmentalists who want the area to be protected from any development. So, each of the environmentalists will pose a concern or make a demand, and the oil people must address their concerns and negotiate with them.

Give the two teams several minutes to discuss their position and try to anticipate the opposition's points in order to be ready to rebut them. When they are ready, or time is up, have them begin. The environmentalists will take turns asking a question or stating a concern. The oil people must listen and respond in a way that satisfies the environmentalist and furthers the project agenda.

Teaching Tips:

Before class, arrange the desks so one side of the classroom is facing the other. The environmentalists can then face the oil people. If this isn't possible, have the students stand to speak.

If the students say they don't know much about environmental issues or they don't know how to respond as a business person, talk a bit about how politicians speak. That should be familiar to them.

Procedure:

1. Before class, arrange the desks so one side of the classroom is facing the other.
2. Divide the class into two groups: environmentalists and oil people.
3. Give the class the scenario (above) and several minutes for each group to discuss their position and try to anticipate the opposition's points in order to be ready to rebut them.
4. Have the environmentalists take turns asking a question or stating a concern.

Reported Speech Activity

Skills: Listening/speaking

Time: 5-10 minutes

Materials: None

Optional materials: Sentence cards, or worksheet/whiteboard/PowerPoint

Reported speech can be difficult for students, so a little regular practice can help make it more automatic. This activity overcomes one of the major hurdles of listening activities in that it gives students a reason to listen closely to their classmates.

Ask student A a question. Ask student B to "report" student A's answer. Model the activity first by asking a student a question and then reporting the answer to the class.

Example:

T: What day is it today?

A: Today is Tuesday.

T: A said today is Tuesday.

As you can see, students have to listen carefully to both the original question and then the answer to the question in order to do the reported speech element. After doing some examples, put students into groups of 3 and let each of them have a turn doing each role (question asker, answerer and reported speech person).

Procedure:

1. Ask one student a question.

2. That student answers the question.

3. Ask another to report the answer to the class.

4. Do a few examples of this and have some forms on the whiteboard for students to refer to if necessary.

5. Put students into groups of 3.

6. Each student can have a few turns doing each role (asking questions, answering questions, reporting the answer).

Infographic Presentation

Skills: Reading/writing/speaking/listening

Time: 1+ hour

Materials: Internet access, PowerPoint

Optional Materials: Video camera

Presentations are a regular feature of ESL classes, but your student may get overwhelmed at the thought of first creating and then presenting a full-length speech. Infographics have become a common way of presenting information, and your student can create and use one to provide the "meat" of an informative oral presentation. This will also provide an opportunity to research a topic in English. If your student works in an office, he or she is likely to use PowerPoint at work, so the combination of something familiar (PPT) with something new (English presentation) should reduce stress.

Have your student choose a topic of interest to them that has several data points. For example, if he/she has a favorite team, he/she can find the team's current ranking, average points per game, number of championships, and so on to populate the infographic. The student should begin the project by researching several data points and finding an image or two online to use for decoration.

To create the infographic, the student will need to reset the margins to create the long, narrow look of an infographic. This is done by choosing a blank layout and changing the slide from landscape to portrait then adjusting the margins. Start with 10"/25cm by 30"/75cm and adjust if necessary. Your student can use images, Smart Art, and/or charts to present the data he/she will report. However, you may want to give your student a time limit for choosing a layout or have him/her make a sketch before opening PowerPoint, because the number of options can become a time waster.

Once the layout has been chosen, your student will need to fill in the data. If he/she is using charts, Excel will automatically to fill them in. Don't worry, it's pretty self-explanatory and the end result is right there for the student to see while working. Once the images are all in place, the student should add a brief explanation of each image. All images and text boxes can be resized, and the entire slide can be resized by adjusting the margins, if there is more (or less) information than expected.

When the student is satisfied with the infographic, it can be saved as a JPEG. This will probably have taken an entire lesson, so the presentation will be in the next lesson. You should tailor the focus of the presentation to your student's level and needs. A lower-level student may just need to practice speaking without a script. Higher-level students may need to practice the use of gestures or inflection.

For the presentation of the infographic, pull up the saved image and have the student sit or stand next to the computer to present the data to you. A lower-level student may do best seated next to you with both of you looking at the screen. Being able to look at the image (and not having you looking directly at your student) should reduce quite a bit of stress. After doing several presentation activities, the student's confidence will hopefully increase and he/she won't need such modifications.

Teaching Tips:

If a student does not use PowerPoint at work and is not familiar with it (or if you do not want to spend an entire lesson making an infographic), you may want to have the student find an existing infographic online to present.

A video of the presentation can be helpful for your student. When students see and hear themselves, they can more easily see the areas that need improvement.

Procedure:

1. Have the student choose a topic of interest that would have several data points to research and present.

2. Have the student make a sketch of the planned infographic.

3. Using PowerPoint, have the student make the infographic (use a blank layout, in portrait, with the margins set to 10"/25cm by 30"/75cm).

4. In the next lesson, have the student present the infographic to you. According to the student's level, have him/her focus on speaking without a script, using gestures, or inflection, etc.

5. Review the presentation.

Group Therapy

Skills: Speaking/listening

Time: 10 minutes

Materials: None

In the style of an AA meeting, students sit in a circle if possible and introduce themselves, "My name is _____, and I'm _____." Instead of finishing with ". . . and I'm an alcoholic," finish with a problem they have learning English, such as using articles correctly or conjugating verbs. They should then solicit tips and tricks from their classmates. The teacher should begin by modeling and could give an actual problem they have as a language student. For example, "My name is Jennifer, and I'm never sure how formal or polite to be when speaking Korean to someone I don't know well. Does anyone have any advice for me?"

Teaching Tip:

This is a great first day activity, because it is a not-very-sneaky way to get an idea of what areas of language the students perceive to be more difficult, which you can use to inform your lesson planning for the semester.

Procedure:

1. Before class, arrange the desks in a circle, if possible. If the class is very large, divide students into several large groups.

2. Begin by telling your students that everyone has trouble learning languages, and even those who speak several languages fluently have difficulty with some aspect of any language they learn.

3. Introduce the lesson as "therapy" for them to get counseling for their troubles.

4. Begin with your own example of a problem you have with a foreign language you speak. For example, "My name is Jennifer, and I'm never sure how formal or polite to be when speaking Korean to someone I don't know well. Does anyone have any advice for me?"

5. Go around the circle and give each student a turn to introduce themselves, "My name is _____, and I'm _____." Instead of finishing with ". . . and I'm an alcoholic," finish with a problem they have learning English, such as using articles correctly or conjugating verbs. They should then solicit tips and tricks from their classmates.

Person on the Street

Skills: Speaking/listening

Time: 10-15+ minutes

Materials: Laminated question cards

In this activity, each student takes a turn as the reporter, asking a current events question from a card, and the group members answer as a man on the street. Begin with a discussion of the news and people on the street interviews, and/or prep a few clips of such interviews (you might include a funny one or two, such as "Jaywalking with Jay Leno"), or clips from ELLLO (www.elllo.org) which are non-native speakers. Divide students into small groups and give each member of the group a different question card—the groups can have the same pool of cards.

Procedure:

1. In advance, prepare question cards with one current events question on each card.

Laminate them, if you want to use them with more than one class. Optionally, also prepare a few clips of people on the street interviews to show a few examples to students.

2. Begin class with a discussion of the news, specifically, person on the street interviews.

3. Explain to the class that they will take turns being a reporter and the person on the street.

4. Divide students into groups of 4-5 and give each group enough question cards for each student to have a different question.

5. 5. If you want this to be a short activity, have each reporter choose a different person on the street, so each group member asks and answers one question each

6. If you want to extend the activity, have a group discussion after about the different opinions on current events held by the class members.

Story Picture Cards Sequencing

Skills: Speaking/listening

Time: 15+ minutes

Materials: Laminated cards which have a sequence of pictures, one per student plus your own

This is an activity better suited to higher level students. In advance, prepare individual pictures which tell a story when put together. Give each student one picture. Without showing one another their pictures, students must discuss the images in order to determine the correct sequence of images which tells a story. When they think they have the correct order, everyone reveals their pictures to see if they are correct.

Teaching Tips:

If the class is very large, have two or even three different sets of pictures, each telling a different story. Clearly mark each set, so students know who they should be working with. This is intended to be a mingling activity, but it could be done in groups while sitting.

Make sure the pictures have elements which lend themselves to easier sequencing, such as a clock, the sun/moon, and activities usually done at a certain time, such as eating, commuting, and working.

The books Zoom and Re-Zoom by Istvan Banyai are perfect for this activity, if you can get your hands on a copy. Just be sure to use a sequence of pages in order.

Procedure:

1. In advance, prepare a series of pictures which tell a story when put in order.
2. Tell students they must discuss their pictures without revealing them to each other, in order to determine the correct sequence of the images.
3. When the students all think they have the correct order, have them reveal their pictures to one another to see if they are correct. The teacher can check answers with the class if necessary.

Human Logic Puzzle

Skills: Listening/speaking/writing

Time: 5-10 minutes

Materials: Flashcards, answers grids

You probably remember logic puzzles from when you were a kid. It begins with a short story followed by clues and a grid for keeping track of the information. In this activity, there are clues but no short story.

In advance, prepare a grid with the terms you want to review. The terms should be listed across the top while blanks for student names should be along the side. With lower-level students, you may want to use this for jobs, animals, actions or other terms the students will be able to provide clues for fairly easily. With higher-level students, you can use a broader variety of vocabulary and they can give synonyms, antonyms and/or definitions.

Before you begin, you need to select student helpers/clue providers to go to the front of the class. Give each two flashcards, and tell them not to show anyone. Give the rest of the students the answer grid and tell them to write the student helpers' names.

In turn, student helpers/clue providers should give one clue about one of their flashcards. For something like jobs, they can describe where the person works, what they do, etc. For animals or actions, they can act it out and/or make noises. Let the students give the first round of clues themselves while subsequent rounds will include audience participation. That is, the "audience" asks questions. Continue until one student has correctly completed his/her grid.

Variations:

To make it more challenging:

1. Limit students to two turns, i.e. one turn per flash card. If no one has correctly completed his/her grid, students could then work in pairs or small groups.

2. Have two columns on the answer sheet, rather than a grid, so students will write the names of the students and the vocabulary they are describing.

To make it less challenging:

1. Have students continue giving more clues until everyone has completed their grid.

2. Have students work in small groups or pairs. Give them 15-20 seconds between clues to discuss.

Procedure:

1. In advance, prepare a grid with the terms you want to review.

2. Select student helpers/clue providers to go to the front of the class and give each of them two flashcards.

3. Give the rest of the class the answer grid and tell them to write the student helpers' names.

4. Have student helpers/clue providers give one clue about one of their flashcards in turn. After they have given one clue about each flashcard, the clues should be

responses to student questions. (You may want to make rules about the questions they can ask.)

5. Give the class time to think and write between each clue.

6. Students continue giving clues until one student has correctly filled out their grid.

Top 10 Tips for Teaching ESL Speaking

Student-Centered vs. Teacher-Centered

When many ESL teachers first start off their time in the classroom, they talk a lot (this is known as a teacher-centered classroom) and way more than they should. If you want your students to get better at speaking in English, they need to be speaking in English for most of the class, ideally at least 90% of it (this is known as a student-centered classroom) if they are at intermediate to high levels of proficiency. The best way to make this happen is to put students in pairs or groups of 3, set up an activity or give them a set of conversation questions and let them get to it. Monitor for errors and offer assistance if required, but don't interfere. If you have lower level students, the teacher-talk time will need to be increased from 10% to 30% or more but you should still try to reduce this percentage as much as possible.

A related note to add about making your classes more student-centered is the need for students to have "processing time. " When you teach them new vocabulary or a grammar concept that they're seeing for only the first or second time, they'll need time to organize and understand that material before they're expected to actively use it. It can be helpful to use some very controlled spoken or written exercises before doing more open-ended activities or games. You'll find that most textbooks are designed in this way—the grammar point or vocabulary is introduced through a reading or listening, students "notice" the language, the teacher "presents" the language (or students do a guided discovery instead), there's a controlled practice with a written exercise, and finally students "produce" the language in a freer activity, either written or spoken.

Teach Students How to Ask Questions

Conversation is a two-way street and in order to be good at it our students need to know how to ask questions. Conversation is not asking and answering something like:

A: "How was your weekend?"

B: "It was good."

149

A better conversation would look like:

A: "How was your weekend?"

B: "It was good, I saw a movie."

A: "Really? **What** movie?"

Or,

A: "How was your weekend?"

B: "It was a bit boring, I just stayed home. **How** about you?"

A: "Oh, mine was fun, I went to _____."

I remind my students of the key question words: who/what/when/why/where/how and tell them that they can almost always use at least a couple of them to ask a follow-up question to their conversation partner. Also, teach your students question forms; it's maybe not as obvious as you think since questions are formed in a variety of grammatical ways in other languages and your students may not know how to make them. For example, even my very advanced level students in Korea still make mistakes with the negative past question forms ("Why didn't you went to work yesterday?" Or, "Why don't you go to work yesterday?"). If you know a little bit about the first language of your students, it can be quite useful in understanding the errors that they're making.

Statements in English often follow the pattern of Subject-Verb-Object (He speaks Italian). There is no auxiliary verb in this statement, so the helping verb "do" is used in the question form (Does he speak Italian?).

If there is an auxiliary verb in the statement, it is inverted with the subject when it is made into a question. For example:

He can speak English. ---> Can he speak English?

These are only the most basic of examples and it can be far more complicated; even high level students are easily confused about how to make the question forms so reviewing them periodically will be useful in helping our students learn how to engage in conversations.

Additionally, an important speaking sub-skill that is useful but which our students often aren't that confident in is initiating a conversation. We can teach them a few strategies, appropriate topics, and useful phrases to help them with this. You will have to use your discretion to know what kinds of questions are appropriate in your particular situation because it can vary so much from country to country.

Listening is Important

It's tempting, even in our first language to not listen to our conversation partner, but instead think of the next witty or wise thing to say in our heads. This does not lead to good conversations. Instead, truly listen to what your partner is saying and then respond to that. I make sure to talk to my students about this because it's even more tempting to do this in a second or third language where you are struggling to put words together into coherent sentences. There are a few tips I tell my students to help them out.

The first and last words in the question are key if it is a "W/H" question. For example, "Where do you go to school?" If you hear *where*, then you know that your answer needs to be a place of some sort and if you hear school, the answer should be quite obvious. "Do you go to" is necessary for forming a grammatically correct question but it's not that important for the listener to be able to answer appropriately. If a student catches the key words, it's possible for them to make a reasonable guess at the correct answer. This tip is also especially useful for something like the TOIEC listening test, where many of the possible answers can be eliminated by knowing what the first word in the question is.

I also teach my students phrases that they can use if they didn't understand the question and missed the key words. For example, they could say something like, "Sorry, could you please repeat the question?" or, "I didn't understand, could you say it again slowly?" I tell them that it's not a terrible thing to ask someone to repeat something and that it's always better than giving a completely random answer that's unrelated to the question.

It Doesn't Always need to be Fun

When you're new to teaching, there is the temptation to always be a constant entertainer. I call these people edutainers. However, edutainer mode is hard to keep up, week after week, month after month, and year after year. While it's good to have a laugh and a joke once in a while, learning English is not easy so it is okay to have more serious kinds of speaking activities that do not involve a game of some sort.

For example, partner conversation activities are extremely valuable because that means that every single student in your class is either listening or talking in a very active way for the duration of that activity. It also gives students a chance to get feedback from a partner similar to their own level, which is helpful because they are able to see if what they are saying is comprehensible, or not. Students will appreciate your classes if their English speaking skills are improving, even if you are not the most entertaining teacher so don't be afraid to do some more serious things.

Make a Plan

Many ESL teachers have a heavy teaching schedule of up to 30 hours/week (or more!), so there often isn't much time or energy to make lesson plans for classes. However, it can be quite challenging to have *consistently* great classes if you don't spend at least a few minutes thinking about the class and jotting down a few ideas about what you're going to do. Even if you have only 5-10 minutes, here are a few things you could think about:

1. How will you introduce the target language? A reading passage? A listening exercise? A story? A worksheet?

2. What will you write on the board?

3. What controlled practice activity will you do? What page in your book? Another resource? Is it student-centered? Could you have students do it with speaking,

instead of writing (if it's a conversation class)? How will you provide feedback?

4. What freer practice activity will you do? Is it student-centered? Are students speaking a lot? How will you provide feedback?

5. What will you do if you have some extra time left at the end of class?

6. Do you need any supplementary materials?

7. Follow-up or review in the next class?

Even spending five minutes jotting down the answer to these seven questions on a blank piece of paper before class will prove extremely useful in reducing your overall stress levels with regards to teaching as well as being beneficial for your students. It will even save you more time if you make a lesson plan template and then print off a stack of them to last you a month or two. Students also feel reassured that they are in capable hands if you have at least a few things written down on a piece of paper because they know you've spent time thinking about the class and that you have a plan for them to follow.

Remember that students see the greatest improvements when they're challenged to do new things, so in this case it would be using new grammar constructions or vocabulary when speaking. If you plan carefully, you can ensure that your students are being pushed to do this, instead of just relying on their regular "go to repertoire" of things they've probably been using for years. Challenging our students could also involve pushing them to use their previous knowledge in a new activity or context and of course, this book is an excellent place to start if you need a few new ideas for speaking activities!

Provide a Demonstration of the Language and Game/Activity

A normal way that people learn a language is by first "seeing" and then "doing. " You can demonstrate the target language to your students in various ways such as using a video clip from a movie, song, podcast, or the MP3 listening files and reading exercises that are in your textbook. Of course, you, the teacher, can also provide an example for your students but it's good for them to hear different genders, accents, and levels of

English speakers so be sure to change it up from time to time. Keep in mind that there are many English speakers in the world who speak English as their second, third or fourth language so be sure to use some of these examples as well.

Another situation in which you'll want to provide a demonstration for your students is when you set up an activity or game. Especially if your students are beginners, it will be extremely difficult for them to understand instructions without seeing a demonstration of them as well. I've found that even with my advanced classes, it is helpful to provide a demonstration because if I don't, my students often end up doing something that I don't want them to be doing. And of course, it's totally my fault!

Change Partners

A common thing that happens in ESL classes is that students sit with the same partner every single day. This is not useful for a number of reasons, the main one being fossilization, where errors get entrenched. One way that our students know they are making a mistake is if their partner is unable to understand them. If a student goes with the same partner each time, that partner will get to know their mistakes and be able to understand them, even if nobody else can which isn't useful. Another reason that you need to change it up is that students are usually more motivated to speak in the target language (English!) if they aren't with their BFF. Finally, it gets boring to talk to the same person over and over again so changing it up periodically will increase motivation in your classes.

Give Feedback

If you hear some errors while students are speaking, it can be helpful to give feedback to them. Think back to your own experiences of learning a language, sport skill or musical instrument. Part of learning is just practicing on your own, but I'm sure there were cases when you got some extremely valuable feedback about an error you were making which accelerated your improvement significantly. Our students want us to give them feedback on the errors that they are making and in my own informal surveys that is what students think my most important role should be.

There are two schools of thought about this: error correction can happen during the activity, or at the end. My general rule is that if you are focusing on accuracy, it is helpful to correct during an activity, especially for the controlled practice activities. If you are focusing on fluency, correct at the end and don't interrupt.

Don't forget that it's not helpful to correct everything unless you have very advanced level students. Doing so will overwhelm your students and destroy their confidence. I will usually correct the following types of errors:

1. Those that impede understanding and communication in a significant way but only if it's something that my students are at a level to understand. For example, maybe a high beginner student doesn't know how to form questions and is asking, "dinner-eat?" It would be helpful to stop and at least write the correct form on the board for the student to copy, "What will _____ _____ tonight?"

2. Those that involve the target language of that lesson.

3. Those that involve something we recently studied together in the past month or two.

4. Those that students at their level should have down cold. For example, a high intermediate level student should not be making any mistakes using the simple past.

Use the Whiteboard for Key Words and Phrases

Just because you showed students some vocabulary or a new grammar concept once or twice doesn't mean that they're going to remember it or be able to recall it when necessary. A way that we can help them is by writing the key vocabulary words or phrases that you are teaching that day on one side of the whiteboard and leave them up there for the entire class for students to refer to if necessary. This is especially important for beginners because they often don't have the scaffolding in place in their brains to connect new material to, as our more advanced level students would. Gradually, as students become more proficient at using those particular words or grammatical constructs, we can stop putting them on the board and challenge students to recall them on their own.

Change it Up

Just because a speaking game or activity worked well in one class, doesn't mean that you should keep using it again and again. This will become boring quickly for your students. Variety is key to keeping our students interested and engaged in the class and it's always good to challenge our students with new things so they can improve their skills.

Before You Go

Before you go, please leave a review wherever you got this book. I appreciate your feedback and it will help other teachers like yourself find this book. My goal is to spread some ESL teaching awesome to the world!

Jackie Bolen around the Internet

ESL Speaking (www.eslspeaking.org)

YouTube (https://www.youtube.com/c/jackiebolen)

Instagram (www.instagram.com/jackie.bolen)

Pinterest (www.pinterest.com/eslspeaking)

Made in United States
Troutdale, OR
03/03/2024